COMPLETELY REVISED EDITION

How to Become

a Good Dancer

by ARTHUR MURRAY

with Dance Secrets by KATHRYN MURRAY

Illustrated by Lealand Gustavson

Simon and Schuster · New York · 1959

LIBRARY OF CONGRESS CATALOG CARD NUMBER: 54-5895
MANUFACTURED IN THE UNITED STATES OF AMERICA

TABLE *of* CONTENTS

The Art of Dancing

THOSE WHO ARE INTERESTED in history know that dancing is one of the oldest and most enduring of all the arts. Primitive people danced to convey their ideas, emotions, beliefs. Later, in ancient Greece and Rome, dancing was used to portray the meaning of ceremonies and rituals. During the Renaissance, dancing took on a social form and became a recreational communication between people.

Actually, through all those years up to today, dancing has not changed in one of its basic aspects. It has always been, and still is, a means of *expression.*

To me, the clearest definition of up-to-date ballroom dancing is *conversation set to music.*

When you dance, you express yourself. You hold a partner's interest through musical rhythm, just as in good conversation you hold a companion's interest through words. A man who leads attractive, well-timed steps is similar to a man who talks well in any social gathering. A girl who can follow is similar to one who spurs on a conversation and is said to be "so easy to talk to and to know."

And, just as speaking knowledge on many subjects makes you

a more interesting talker, *dancing knowledge* of a variety of steps and tempos makes you a more interesting dancer. The more skill you acquire, the more "words" you will have for your dancing conversations.

A foreigner who has not learned a language has difficulty in making himself understood. He tries so hard to *think* of the right words that he stammers and hesitates.

And so it is with dancing. If you are too busy *thinking* about each step, if you are uncertain and timid about trying, you can't express yourself freely. There will be too many things on your mind for you to be yourself. And being yourself — gracefully, rhythmically — is the whole secret of good dancing.

To be a good dancer, you must be able to dance without having to concentrate on the steps. Your feet must have learned to respond easily and smoothly to the music. You must be able to lead or follow without apparent effort. And this final stage of perfection is reached in only one way: Learn — and practice!

I have arranged the instructions in this book so that you will have no difficulty progressing in easy stages. But before you begin, I want to add this advice: Do not skip any of the material in the early pages because it looks too easy. Even if you have danced before, basic instructions will prove to be valuable as review. Start at the beginning — not in the middle of the book.

Once you know how to dance really well, you will never forget what you have learned. And, since there is no age limit in dancing, you can enjoy that happy recreation for the rest of your life.

How to Become

a Good Dancer

Part One

THE FIRST STEP

Why Good Dancers are Popular

IT'S EASY to understand why good dancers are in demand. Just watch any crowd on a ballroom floor. Those who can dance well look happy — in tune with the gaiety and the music. Not only are they enjoying themselves but their partners are having a fine time, too.

We dance because it's fun; that's reason enough. But dancing is also an easy and delightful form of exercise. Good dancers have a vigorous youthful posture, supple grace and superb muscle tone. People like to dance; they are born with a deep love of moving to rhythm.

Anyone Can Learn to Dance

I HAVE NEVER met a normal person who could not become a fine dancer. You have the same natural ability others have and good dancing is within your reach. But remember — you can't learn to dance by reading. You'll have to practice. So don't just skim through these pages. Learn each step thoroughly before you go on to the next.

First, learn to do each routine slowly, without music. Dance alone. When you can do a dance pattern easily and with perfect confidence, try it to slow music. After an hour's practice, try the step to fast music. Do not attempt dancing with a partner until you can do your own part in time to fast music and with complete ease.

Why You Should Learn to Dance Alone at First

DANCING is a muscular exercise and, as with all such activity, calls for smoothly co-ordinated movement. This takes repetition of action to attain, and until you do practice sufficiently your muscles cannot perform with ease and grace. Your movements will be heavy and labored.

If you were just beginning to learn a muscular sport like tennis, it would not be fair to subject anyone but a teacher to playing with you. Until you had perfected your strokes and could run lightly about the court concentrating on the game itself, you would not be much fun as a partner. It is the same with dancing. Until you know your step patterns and can concentrate on the rhythm of the music, neither you nor your partner can enjoy your dancing.

A beginner in dancing has one great advantage over one who is learning a partnership sport. For you *can* learn to dance alone — without a teacher, a relative or a friend to help you. I can give you definite reassurance about this because thousands of men and women have learned to dance through my printed instructions. I have spent many years perfecting this method and if you will follow it, page by page, you will have your full share of the pleasure and happiness which every good dancer enjoys.

Should there be any instructions that you do not understand, you may stop in at your nearest Arthur Murray Studio for complimentary advice.

How to Use the Step Diagrams

YOU WILL SOON BE STARTING to learn the actual steps in Fox Trot and all the other ballroom dances. You will do this through the printed instructions on each page plus, with most steps, a *diagram* showing the exact pattern that your feet should follow.

All body motions in dancing are governed entirely by the movement of your feet and the placement of your weight. Those are the only two factors on which you need concentrate in order to acquire correct dancing appearance. Don't strive for graceful motions by swaying from the waist or moving your head or shoulders. If the step you are learning calls for a turn of the body or shoulder movement, that will come automatically, without conscious thought, through the way you move your feet and place your weight.

All diagrams include a starting position drawn and labeled similar to this:

Always place your feet together, as shown in the drawing, at the start of the step.

Note that the left foot illustration is white; the drawing for the right foot is tinted gray. Thus it will be easy for you to follow the left and right foot movements in even the most advanced steps.

PLACEMENT OF WEIGHT:

Whenever you take a step of any kind, as indicated by a numbered left or right footprint, *always place your weight on that foot*. This is important!

The only time you do not place your weight on the foot that you move is when the footprint is drawn in a dotted line. In such case, you merely touch your foot to the floor as the pattern indicates and retain your weight on the standing foot. This is how the dotted footprint looks:

Before Following a Diagram

REMEMBER THAT THE INSTRUCTIONS on the page will tell you, in full, exactly what to do. The diagrams and illustrations are given as an additional aid to help you to visualize and follow the written instructions. So, before starting a new pattern:

Read all printed instructions.
Study the footprints to picture the pattern mentally as you will be doing it.
Memorize the way to count the step.
Still seated, imagine your feet following the pattern to the rhythmic count given.

Do not stand and try the step until you have a completely clear image of it in your mind. Then place the open book on a nearby table or chair and refer to it to check your own progress.

How to Practice a New Step

As MENTIONED EARLIER, it takes repetition before your muscles can achieve smooth, flowing motions. After you have followed the step pattern to the counts specified —

Repeat the step, without music, at least a dozen times. Do not repeat continuously — start with feet together each time. Count aloud.

When you are sure of the pattern, try repeating it continuously, still without music, as you progress around the room.

Now turn on your music, using a slow tempo of whichever dance you are learning. *Count with the music* before starting to dance to it.

After you are able to dance the step, in continuous repetition to slow music, try it to a faster tempo. (Ability to learn differs; the average student needs a half hour's practice to slow music and twenty to thirty minutes' practice to fast music.)

How to Progress Around a
Dance Floor

THE LINE OF DIRECTION

THERE IS A STANDARD RULE for progressing around any dance floor, and if you adhere to it there is less chance of your bumping into other couples. It is called the Line of Direction and it means to move counterclockwise — in other words, *opposite* to the way that the hands of a clock travel.

Here is an illustration of the Line of Direction:

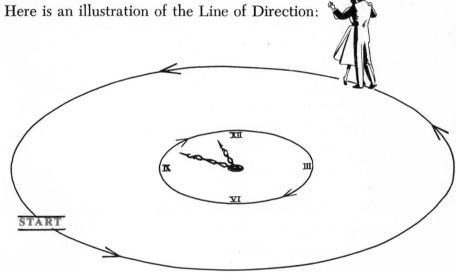

When you are learning a new step pattern and practicing it with continuous repetition, do so by following the Line of Direction.

PRACTICE IN THIS WAY:

The man progresses forward around the room with his right hand nearest the wall. The girl starts backward with her left hand nearest the wall.

How to Keep Time to Music and Develop Your Sense of Rhythm

THERE IS A MISTAKEN IMPRESSION that it is necessary to be able to "carry a tune" in order to learn how to keep time to music. This unfortunate belief keeps many people from learning to dance.

The ability to carry a tune is not a necessary factor in learning to dance. To dance, you must simply be able *to keep time to music.* And if you can march to band music, or if your foot can beat time to ordinary dance music, you have a good enough sense of rhythm to enjoy dancing.

Everyone was born with a sense of rhythm. Forget that you must know music — nine out of ten dancers don't know one note from another, yet they can keep time.

IF YOU CAN CARRY A TUNE:

If you can sing, hum, or whistle a tune — *any* tune, whether it is a popular dance number, a nursery lullaby or "Yankee Doodle" — then you have already proved that you have sufficient rhythm to become a good dancer.

IF YOU CAN'T CARRY A TUNE:

Remember this: Dancers do not keep time to the melody or the tune of a song. The high and low notes have nothing to do with it. The count in dancing is determined by the *beat* or tempo of the music.

If you are standing at the curb when a parade band passes by, you automatically *feel* the beat and tempo of the march being played. The "oompah-oompah" of the big brass horns and the "boom, boom, boom-boom-boom" of the big bass drum arouse in you a regular, rhythmic *pulse*. Your muscles automatically get ready to swing you off in perfect step with the rest of the parade!

The same principle is true of dance music. When you hear a popular song played on the radio or phonograph, you cannot help feeling the underlying tempo, or beat, or pulse, of the music. If an orchestra is playing, this beat is usually carried by the bass drum. As you listen, shut your eyes and visualize the drummer's foot working the pedal of that drum. At each beat his foot goes down, and a soft "boom" accents the tempo.

These accented or "boom" beats are all you need for dancing. To make sure that you recognize them (if there still is any question in your mind), do these two things:

1. *Beat Time With Your Foot.*

Sit next to your radio or phonograph and listen to any dance music. Imagine that you are the drummer and simply beat time with your foot on the floor as though you were hitting the pedal of the bass drum. Tap your hand on the chair arm at the same time. Keep tapping to different types of music until it becomes automatic to follow the drumbeat.

2. *Walk in Time to Music.*

After you have learned to beat time, walk around the room, taking one step to each beat. Do this in private, so that you will not feel self-conscious. Try walking to several different songs. In a surprisingly short while, your feet will "carry the tune" easily.

And that's all there is to keeping time with the music!

In following chapters I will tell you how this applies to each dance; but the same simple principle applies to them all.

The Walking Step in Dancing

FROM THE VERY FIRST STEP PATTERNS that you learn, you will be told to walk forward or back.

It is easy to learn to walk gracefully, in time to the music, if you read these pointers carefully and follow them.

While you are learning, practice by walking only on the ball of the foot. You must emphasize this at the start; then when you become proficient your walking steps will be light and comfortable.

Lift your feet slightly off the floor in all walking steps. To slide or scrape your feet will make you feel heavy.

All forward and backward walking steps are taken with the body erect but with weight held forward.

As you walk forward or backward, let the toes point the way. Touch the floor with your toes first.

In all dance steps, including walking steps, stretch from the ankle as you let your toes lead.

How to Prepare
for Partnership Dancing
While Practicing Alone

ALTHOUGH YOU SHOULD LEARN your own part thoroughly before attempting to dance with anyone, there is no reason to lose sight of your real goal, that of partnership dancing.

So, as you learn step patterns and practice them, look to the future, when you will be dancing with a variety of partners. For a man this means holding his partner correctly so that he can lead her; for a girl, standing correctly and developing ease of motion so that she will be able to follow. Therefore, during your practice alone, adopt regular dance position — with your arms and body held as in ballroom dancing. *Practice with an imaginary partner.*

How to Hold a Partner

THERE IS NOTHING mysterious about "how to hold your partner" in dancing. Your position should be guided by comfort, common sense and convention — and that is all there is to it.

Outside of a few eccentric crazes like the Bunny Hug, Charleston, Black Bottom and so on, position in ballroom dancing hasn't changed appreciably in the past thirty years.

Youngsters have always had fads in their dancing style. One year you may find young girls leaving their right arms outstretched, palms up, as though feeling for raindrops. By the next season they will have forgotten that fad and will adopt another distinctive style.

Some youngsters assume exaggerated dancing positions merely to cover their embarrassment at not knowing what to do. As their dancing improves, they will drop affectations. Young people are more comfortable when they dance exactly as their friends do; wise parents realize this and overlook short-lived styles.

In this book we are concerned only with presenting to you the quickest and easiest means of becoming a good dancer, popular with all partners. A correct dancing position will help to make this possible.

TEN RULES FOR A CORRECT DANCING POSITION

1. You can practice correct dancing position very easily in your own room, without a partner. Face a mirror and stand erect. Don't strain — simply stand naturally and comfortably as though you were about to walk down the street. Now rise so that your weight is placed evenly on the soles of your shoes — no weight on your heels. Hum a popular tune and walk about in time to the rhythm until you feel fully at ease.

2. You will find it helpful to raise your arms in typical dancing position as you practice alone. Do not hold your elbows unnaturally high — it is tiring, unnecessary and out of date. Glance in the mirror and you will see that a medium elbow height forms the most graceful line.

Don't hold your elbows
unnaturally high.

3. Looking at yourself standing erect, with your arms up, will
   remind you to hold yourself tall. Good dancing posture is
   flattering. It will help you to form the habit of holding
   your head high, with your chest out and chin in. Bring out
   the best in your looks!
4. Keep your heels off the floor as much as possible. A flat-
   footed, firm stance belongs on the golf course, not on the
   dance floor. Keeping your weight over the balls of your
   feet will make you feel quicker and lighter as a partner.
5. Keep your feet close together, unless you are taking a definite
   step to the side. This is one of the most important things
   for you to remember. Without this, you can never hope to
   be a good dancer or even to "get by" in appearance. Walk
   toward your mirror in dance position with your feet apart.
   It's not a pretty sight, is it? Now, walk again and make a

conscious effort to pass your feet closely together. Are you sold on why this is so important in dancing?

Stepping with feet apart is WRONG. Whether stepping forward or back, keep feet moving along a straight line.

Keeping feet together is RIGHT. Here is a short step, with feet together. Practice until you can take a *long* step, forward or back, keeping feet in a straight line.

6. For graceful dancing, you must learn to turn your toes out, rather than in. Again, a peek at your mirror will convince you why this looks better.

7. When dancing with someone, adopt the most comfortable position for both of you. Not so close together that you have no freedom of movement, but not too far apart.

8. The man's right arm is held at the level that is most comfortable according to his height and that of his partner. The girl should take a firm hold with her *left* hand just in back of the man's right shoulder.

Both partners should stand comfortably erect and close enough to one another so that each step is easily followed.

9. A man leads best when he holds his partner almost directly in front of him, just a bit to his right. He can then look ahead, over her right shoulder.

10. Don't lean forward or backward; just assume a natural, comfortable position and your partner will find you a natural, comfortable dancing companion.

The Secrets of Leading

A MAN who is learning to dance alone must first learn his step patterns. When he can follow the instructions easily, in time to the music, he should practice as though he were leading a partner to dance with him.

Here are facts for a man to remember:

The dance floor is the one place where the weaker sex prefers to remain submissive. Girls expect their partners to set the pace — to choose and direct the steps. All that they ask of you is a definite indication of where you are heading.

To give this definite indication, a man must first be clearly certain of just what he does want to do. If he himself is not sure, how can he expect a partner to be able to follow him? There is no short cut to good leading. It takes a definite, well-defined knowledge of the steps.

So the foremost rule is: Know the steps! Then you will move

with assurance, and your partners will feel confidence in your ability.

Believe it or not, a girl does not need to be pushed, pulled or hauled to make her go your way. When you can do your own part well, you won't have to worry about leading. Reserve your strong-arm tactics for other times, other places than the dance floor.

Sometimes, when dancing with a brand-new partner who can follow but is not yet familiar with your style of dancing, you may have to do a bit of guiding. This is done with your right hand and arm. Always hold your right hand firmly just above your partner's waist; you will find that she will respond easily to a light pressure. Your left hand does very little toward leading.

Pointers for Good Leaders

1. Don't be afraid to pause, in position with your partner, at the beginning of each dance. Listen to the music and make sure of your timing before you start forward.

2. When dancing with a new partner for the first time, start off with very simple steps. You then become acquainted with each other's style in dancing.

3. Most good dancers lead the same step at least twice in succession. It makes their dancing more flowing — and it gives them time to plan a graceful sequence to their pattern of steps. It is far better to do the same step several times than rush into quick, jerky changes.

4. Never count for your partner unless you don't care what she thinks of you. Neither is it necessary for you to tell her, in words, what you expect to do next. Knowing your own

part well and holding your right hand firmly on her back
will convey a sufficient message to her.

Don't extend your arm too rigidly.

Further Hints for the Man

1. There is a logical reason for a man's left arm to be extended while he dances. It is held out so as to avoid collisions with other couples as you dance by. But your arm does not have to extend as rigidly and inflexibly as a bumper, nor does your elbow have to be held at an uncomfortably sharp angle. Simply hold the girl's hand lightly but firmly with your left arm in an easy, graceful curve.

2. As you dance, look over the girl's right shoulder. By holding your partner directly in front of you or a bit to your right, you will have a clear view of what's ahead. You are the leader, so it is up to you to choose a clear path.

3. Hold your partner firmly enough to guide her. A weak, listless hold will not inspire her confidence in you. Hold your hand at a comfortable height on the middle of her back.

4. Always start your first step forward with your left foot. Let your toes lead and step directly toward your partner's right foot. Don't worry, she'll be moving hers backward.

WHICH IS A RIGHT TURN, AND WHICH IS A LEFT?

This is a question that sometimes is a little confusing to a beginner. To help you recognize the two turns quickly, here are two aids to turning in the proper direction:

This Is a Right Turn

To make a right turn, look over your right shoulder and let the rest of your body follow.

A man should be guided by this same rule, and to lead a right turn he moves his left hand forward.

And This Is a Left

To make a left turn, look over your left shoulder and let the rest of your body follow.

To lead a left turn, move the left hand backward.

The Secret of Following

I ONCE MET a girl who was very unhappy. She said to me, "I don't understand it, Mr. Murray; boys never cut in on me but I know I can dance — why, I can follow anyone." I danced with her and found that she could follow, provided that I led her in the few simple steps with which she was familiar. As soon as I attempted anything more advanced, she was at a complete loss.

I asked her, "Do most of your partners do these same steps I've been doing with you?"

"Why, yes," she said. "That's exactly the way they dance."

So I explained that her partners were held down. They could do only those few steps because those were all she could follow. I showed her that I could not lead her in any of my other steps without having her falter or stumble.

That girl is only one of the many girls and women who believe that they can follow anyone, and then they wonder why they are not in demand as partners.

A man is limited in his dancing to what his partner can do. He finds it dull and uninteresting when he is hampered in his choice of steps by his partner's lack of knowledge.

Why Girls Also Must Know the Steps

A GIRL CANNOT DANCE with her partner until she knows what she is doing. She can test her own knowledge by trying to dance alone to music or by leading a girl partner. If she feels helpless by herself, she can tell immediately that she does not know her own part. It will be safer for her to refuse invitations until she has learned what she needs to make her popular and fun to have as a partner.

Once a girl becomes interested in the steps themselves, she will enjoy learning. She will begin to notice and pick up pointers from the dancing she sees on the stage, in the movies and on television. She will watch the best dancers among her circle of friends and see steps that she will want to try. The more steps a girl knows, the more freedom and spontaneity she can show in her dancing.

How a Girl Should Study the Steps in This Book

1. When starting a new pattern, first read the instructions for the man's part. It will be easier for you to visualize your own part if you have a clear picture of the direction in which your partner will be moving.
2. Try the man's part of the step.

   A man starts most step patterns by walking forward. Since it is more natural to step forward than back, you will find his part easier to learn. Then when you study your own part, you will be able to pick it up quickly.
3. After trying the man's pattern, read all printed instructions for your own part and study your own diagram.

   By memorizing the footwork and the count, you will be able to try the pattern without holding the book in your hand. Merely refer to the book to check for correctness.
4. Review page 18, which gives full details for practicing step patterns.

Essential Footwork for Girls

A GIRL who is a popular partner can dance with any man — short, tall, one who takes small steps and one who uses long strides.

In order to achieve this ability, *a girl should learn to match her steps to the tallest partner she may meet.* She will then find it easy to adjust to short men or to those of average height.

The trick of taking a long, graceful-looking step is: Stretch from the ankle and let the big toe lead.

When practicing alone, a girl should exaggerate her footsteps to train the muscles of her feet and ankles. It is easy to do this when stepping forward or to the sides; it takes a great deal of practice to become well accustomed to long backward steps. But men dance forward most of the time, so a girl must step backward to put her best foot forward on the dance floor!

Here is an average-length back step taken from the ankle, with the big toe leading. In order to achieve this easily, practice using a step *twice as long.*

THIS POSITION IS WRONG

It is absolutely impossible for a girl to dance well when her feet are placed flat on the floor. In this position her steps will be short and her partner will be unable to move ahead with a long, free, easy dancing stride.

Not only will she be a heavy handicap to her partner, but her feet will appear large and clumsy on the floor.

THIS POSITION IS RIGHT

Note that when the toes lead, a girl's step becomes long and free-moving and that her foot looks graceful.

Here is an easy trick: Imagine that you want to point the way in every step with your one big toe. Let it lead whichever way you move. REACH WITH YOUR TOE, stretching from the ankle — not from the hip.

The Secret of Good Balance for Girls

GOOD BALANCE is the ability to maintain your equilibrium easily, lightly. If you have ever noticed a small child toddling about, you have seen that it takes time before a steady, upright walk is achieved. We learn to balance our weight through practice.

Before we go on, suppose you try this simple balance test. Place your weight on the toes of one foot, raising the other foot off the floor for several inches, either forward or backward. Do you feel steady? Most people cannot hold this pose for more than a few seconds without wavering.

Try the "balance test" again, placing your weight on the toes of one foot, with the other foot extended in air. Now place your left hand on the top of your dresser or on the back of a chair. It's easy to stand steadily now, isn't it?

When you dance, train yourself to hold your left hand very firmly on the back of your partner's shoulder. Don't be afraid, you will not seem heavy. He will not feel the slightest discomfort from that pressure. Instead, you will seem lighter to him.

Why Learning to Lead
Will Help a Girl's Dancing

IF YOU ARE like most girls and women, you will be surprised when you read this: To be a better dancer, learn to lead!

But here is a simple test that may help to convince you. Think back to the girls you knew at school. Select those girls who were in demand at every dance — the girls who had plenty of cut-ins, who were never wallflowers. Now, think it over — weren't they the ones who could lead the other girls as partners?

I first hit upon this theory many years ago. The idea of teaching girls to lead was completely contrary to the accepted beliefs of the day. However, I was sure of the logic and common sense in back of my theory and I decided to try it out.

I visited classes that we held in girls' clubs, schools and colleges. I asked the members of each group to vote for the best dancers among their girl friends. Without a single exception, every good dancer who was chosen was a girl who could lead! Frankly, it has taken a great deal of courage to uphold my strong convictions. Most women cling tenaciously to the belief that "leading will ruin a girl's dancing." It usually takes me a long time to convince mothers that their daughters can become popular dancing partners more quickly by first learning to lead other girls.

The Arthur Murray girl teachers are noted for their ability to follow any partner. The first step in their training is to learn to lead all partners in all dances. In our studios we now teach all girl pupils to lead in addition to teaching them to follow.

So if you have a girl friend or a woman member of your family who would also like to learn to be a good dancer, practice the steps with her.

TWO REASONS WHY LEARNING TO LEAD WILL MAKE A GIRL A BETTER DANCER

1. Have you ever skated hand in hand? If so, you know that it is fun only when you and your partner strike out and glide at the same moment. If one of you is slower and misses the rhythm, twosome skating becomes boring and uncomfortable.

Dancing with a partner works on the same principle. A girl must dance with her partner, not after him. She must express herself in time with the music, not wait woodenly and lifelessly, depending on a strong push-and-pull lead. A girl who can lead understands the music and she can step out rhythmically, at exactly the same time as her partner. Any man will enjoy her dancing because it feels alert, alive, vital.

2. Once a girl can lead, she begins to realize and appreciate the man's part. She discovers what she is expected to do when she is following a partner. A girl who can lead the man's part in any step will be able to follow that step twice as lightly and twice as well. To dance with true poise and assurance, you need the confidence that knowledge brings. Learn to lead each step as well as to follow it.

EXCEPTIONS TO LEADING FOR A GIRL

In all fairness to the old-fashioned prejudice against girls leading, there are certain exceptions to the rule. But it is only in these two cases that leading will be a drawback to a girl's dancing:

1. A girl should not lead another girl more than half the time. The two girls should take equal turns. Sometimes tall girls are forced into leading too often merely because of their height. They should single out other tall girls with whom to practice.

   On the other hand, short girls should not forgo the benefits of leading simply because their friends tower above them. It is a bit harder to lead someone much taller than yourself, but it is not really difficult; it will seem easy with practice. A short man dislikes dancing with a tall girl — not because it is difficult, but because he is afraid that the difference in size will make him look comic. A short girl has nothing to fear on this score; she should feel confident of being able to lead any girl partner.

2. A girl will gain nothing from leading if she leads the same few steps all of the time. Her muscles will become accustomed to only these few movements, and habit will force her into the same steps no matter how strongly her partner leads. She will be in a rut and she will feel stiff and heavy to a man partner.

To gain the full value from leading, a girl must practice leading as many steps as she hopes to be able to follow.

Ten Rules for Following

1. Know the basic steps and their possible combinations. Isn't it logical that you will dance better when you are familiar with the steps a man will do?

2. Give your partner a feeling of freedom in his forward steps — keep your feet out of his way. Develop a long, free, backward step by practicing repeatedly. Dance backward in the Line of Direction, with your left hand nearer the wall.

3. Always let your toes lead. Look at your foot in the mirror as you take a moderate walking step. Now watch what happens when you stretch with your toes. It is a simple matter of arithmetic; you can add actual inches to your step merely by pointing your toes. Practice a long, graceful stride backward, forward and to each side, letting your big toe point the way.

4. Dance on your toes when you practice alone, to strengthen the muscles of your feet.

5. Be ready to move lightly with each step that your partner will take. Don't let your feet cling to the floor or slide along; lift and pass them through the air instead.

6. Avoid short steps when you practice. A small step may seem dainty to you but it will spell disaster to your dancing.

Prove this to yourself by leading one of your girl friends. Tell her to take short steps — it will convince you immediately why you need to develop a long dancing stride.

7. Always be ready to take your first step backward with your right foot. A man steps forward on his left; give him a chance to get going.

8. When you practice alone, hold your arms in partnership dancing position. This will train your arm muscles and insure you against being a weight to a partner.

9. Remember that the secret of good balance while dancing is to take a firm hold with your left hand just in back of a man's right shoulder.

10. If you have a girl friend with whom you can practice, learn to lead each other. Leading will add expression to your dancing — will make you *follow* alertly and with rhythmic ability!

A Man Should Review These Ten Dancing Pointers

1. A man must know his step patterns so thoroughly that he can move to music without concentrating on footwork. Only then can he lead a partner!
2. When learning a new step, read all instructions carefully. Then study the diagram before trying it.
3. First practice a new step without music, counting aloud. Then try it to slow tempo before practicing to faster music.
4. When you can dance a step with continuous repetition, move around the room in the Line of Direction. Your right hand will be nearer the wall.
5. Practice all steps with erect posture, keeping your weight on the balls of your feet. Let your toes lead.
6. Avoid sliding your feet along the floor. Lift them to develop a lighter step. Exaggerate this while practicing until you can dance with ease in any direction.
7. When practicing to music, listen carefully to the beat of the rhythm before starting.
8. Always start forward with your left foot.
9. Remember that you will be holding your partner almost in front of you, a bit to your right. You will be looking over her right shoulder to avoid bumping others.

10. Practice as though you were actually leading a partner. Hold your arms in comfortable partnership position and imagine that you are guiding a girl with your right arm and hand.

Part Two

THE FOX TROT

The Fox Trot

WE ARE NOW READY for the Fox Trot, which is unquestionably the most popular dance throughout the world. Ninety per cent of all popular songs are written in Fox Trot rhythm.

The Fox Trot is not only the most useful of all ballroom dances but it is also the easiest to learn. The majority of popular Fox Trot steps are based on two simple dancing elements. These are:

1. THE WALKING STEP (forward and backward)
2. THE CHASSÉ (or side step)

The name Chassé is one of the very few technical terms that you will find in this book. I have included it because it is in common use. To do a Chassé means to step to the side with one foot and then bring your other foot next to it. A Chassé may be danced to the left or to the right.

Right from the start of your Fox Trot instructions, you will be using forward and backward walking steps in combination with Chassés or side steps. When you have mastered these motions and can also dance them while turning, you will find that the Fox Trot affords a fascinating rhythmic pattern with exciting and engrossing variety.

The Magic Step

AFTER THIRTY YEARS of experience, I hit upon a discovery that changed our entire system of teaching the Fox Trot. I found that *one* easy step was the basis for 75 per cent of all popular Fox Trot steps. Once a person masters the rhythm of this *one* step, it can be used in twenty-seven different ways. So I called this the Magic Step — because the rhythm works like magic!

Before I discovered the Magic Step rhythm, all variations of the Fox Trot had to be learned separately. All combinations had different counts which a pupil had to memorize.

But now, with the Magic Step, you merely learn one rhythmic pattern of two slow and two quick counts which very quickly becomes almost automatic. The music seems to guide you without your thinking, What shall I do next?

The Magic Step pattern itself may be taken forward or backward, and, since it is such a valuable short cut to good Fox Trot dancing, I advise you to spend ample time in learning and practicing it. The Magic Step alone can start a beginner well ahead toward the goal of good dancing.

NOTE: In all Fox Trot variations that use the slow, slow, quick, quick count, *the quick steps are taken twice as fast as the slow.*

The Forward Magic Step

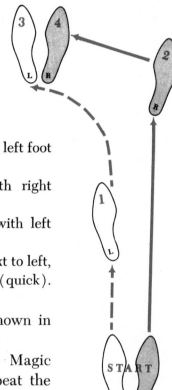

MAN'S PART

START

1. Walk forward with left foot (slow).
2. Walk forward with right foot (slow).
3. Step to left side with left foot (quick).
4. Bring right foot next to left, weight on right (quick).

Start with feet together as shown in the diagram.

After you have learned the Magic Step, try it to slow music. Repeat the step as you progress around the room in the correct Line of Direction, with your right hand nearer the wall. Count slow, slow, quick, quick.

When you are sure of yourself, dance the Magic Step repeatedly to faster music.

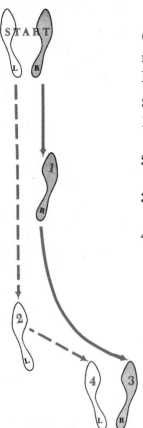

GIRL'S PART when a man leads the Magic Step Forward

START

1. Walk *back* with right foot (slow).
2. Walk *back* with left foot (slow).
3. Step to *right* side with right foot (quick).
4. Bring left foot next to right, weight on left (quick).

GIRLS: First study the man's part of the Magic Step to visualize the pattern. Now study your part. Note that you will start with feet together, ready to move backward with your right foot.

After learning your part, practice by repeating the step, moving backward around the room in the Line of Direction, which means that your left hand will be nearer the wall. Count: Slow, slow, quick, quick.

IMPORTANT: I strongly recommend that you learn this and the following dance steps by yourself. Don't try dancing them with anyone else until you are sure that you know your own part first.

The Magic Step Backward

THE MAGIC STEP BACKWARD has the same count that you have already used when going forward: Slow, slow, quick, quick. But it takes longer to learn to dance backward than forward. Give yourself ample practice — first without music.

MAN'S PART

START

1. Walk back with left foot (slow).
2. Walk back with right foot (slow).
3. Step to left side with left foot (quick).
4. Bring right foot next to left, weight on right (quick).

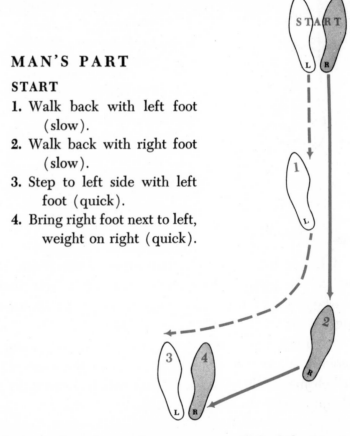

Later, when you have learned to turn, you will find the Magic Step Backward to be a useful pattern in itself. But, in the meantime, study and practice it. You will be using it in your next lesson, the Senior Walk.

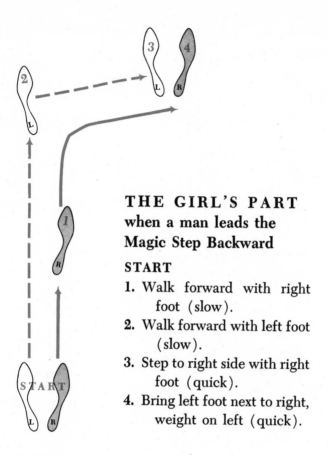

THE GIRL'S PART
when a man leads the Magic Step Backward

START

1. Walk forward with right foot (slow).
2. Walk forward with left foot (slow).
3. Step to right side with right foot (quick).
4. Bring left foot next to right, weight on left (quick).

Start with feet together, ready to move *forward* on your right foot.

Take long walking steps forward on the first two counts, with toes leading as you stretch from the ankle. Keep your feet in a close parallel line. Take a shorter step to the side and follow the curve for footstep 3 that is shown in the diagram. Count aloud: Slow, slow, quick, quick.

The Senior Walk

THIS ADDS TURNS to a forward and backward Magic Step to make an interesting variation.

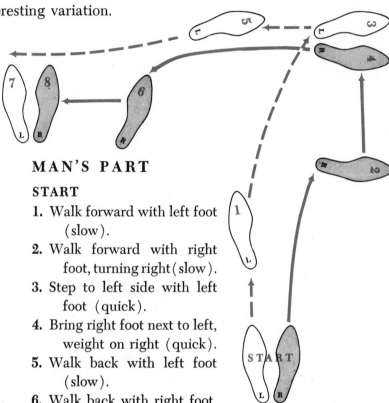

MAN'S PART

START

1. Walk forward with left foot (slow).
2. Walk forward with right foot, turning right (slow).
3. Step to left side with left foot (quick).
4. Bring right foot next to left, weight on right (quick).
5. Walk back with left foot (slow).
6. Walk back with right foot, turning left (slow).
7. Step to left side with left foot (quick).
8. Bring right foot next to left, weight on right (quick).

Note that you turn *right* on the second slow count of the Forward Magic Step and that you turn *left* on the second slow count of the Back Magic Step.

Review "Which Is a Right Turn, and Which Is a Left?" on page 33.

GIRL'S PART when a man leads the Senior Walk

START

1. Step back with right foot (slow).
2. Step back with left foot, turning right (slow).
3. Step to right side with right foot (quick).
4. Bring left foot next to right, weight on left (quick).
5. Walk forward with right foot (slow).
6. Walk forward with left foot, turning left (slow).
7. Step to right side with right foot (quick).
8. Bring left foot next to right, weight on left (quick).

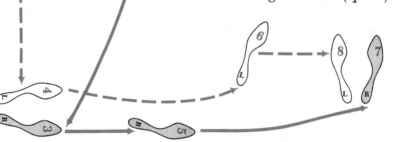

First read the man's instructions on the facing page. This will give you a clearer picture of the over-all pattern of the step. Then study your own part.

When you have learned the girl's part and you are ready to repeat it continuously for practice, do so in the Line of Direction. Start backward around the room with your left hand nearer to the wall.

The Magic Left Turn

HERE AGAIN you have the Magic Step count of slow, slow, quick, quick.

MAN'S PART

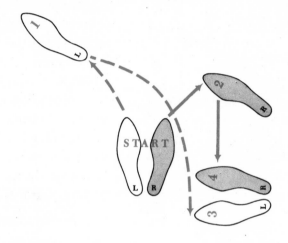

START

1. Walk forward with left foot, turning left (slow).
2. Step back on right foot, still turning *left* (slow).
3. Step to left side with left foot (quick).
4. Bring right foot next to left, weight on right (quick).

The Magic Left Turn is a very useful step. By repeating it in succession, you can make a complete turn to finish as you started, in the Line of Direction.

GIRL'S PART when a man leads the Magic Left Turn

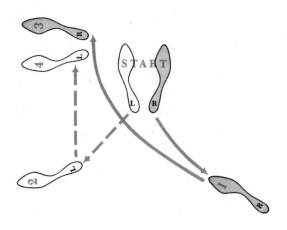

START

1. Step back with right foot, turning left (slow).
2. Step *forward* with left foot, still turning left (slow).
3. Step to right side with right foot (quick).
4. Bring left foot next to right, weight on left (quick).

REMINDER: Always study the man's part first.

After learning your part of the Magic Left Turn, practice it by repeating the pattern just twice. Then stop and again repeat two times. This will avoid dizziness from the unaccustomed turns.

Triple Chassés with Magic Left Turn

IN THE FIRST PART of this pattern, there are three side-and-close steps. Each of these is called a Chassé and the three Chassés total six quick counts.

After you have practiced the three Chassés, add the Magic Left Turn described on the preceding page.

MAN'S PART of the Triple Chassés

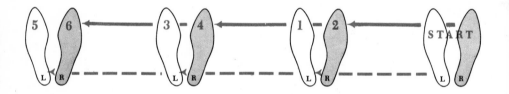

START

1. Step to left side with left foot (quick).
2. Bring right foot next to left, weight on right (quick).

Repeat this action for quick counts **3, 4, 5** and **6.**

After count 6, add the Magic Left Turn danced slow, slow, quick, quick.

GIRL'S PART when a man leads
Triple Chassés with Magic Left Turn

ON THE FACING PAGE are the instructions for the man's part of this pattern. Read them carefully.

Here is your footwork for the first portion of the pattern — the Triple Chassés taken to six quick counts.

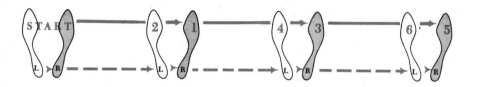

START

1. Step to right side with right foot (quick).
2. Bring left foot next to right, weight on
   left (quick).

Repeat this action for quick counts **3, 4, 5** and **6.**

After you have mastered the three Chassés and can dance them lightly, in time to the music, add the girl's part of the Magic Left Turn.

The Junior Walk

THE JUNIOR WALK is a variation of the Senior Walk and it is an exceptionally attractive-looking step due to the flowing movement of the dance.

First review the Senior Walk, pages 58 and 59. Then, using the same footwork, add this advanced styling:

1. On the two slow forward steps, the man holds his partner far to his right side. This is called a Right Parallel position. See the top illustration on the facing page.
2. On the two slow backward steps (counts five and six) the man holds his partner far to his left side. This is called a Left Parallel position. See the lower illustration on the facing page.

GIRLS: To follow a man who is leading the Junior Walk, use exactly the same footwork that you practiced for the Senior Walk. It will be up to the man to lead you into Junior Walk dance position.

1

2

The Conversation Step

THIS IS a very popular variation of the Magic Step Fox Trot rhythm of slow, slow, quick, quick. First learn the step as diagrammed. Notice that you will be progressing to the side. Then read the instructions at the bottom of the page.

MAN'S PART

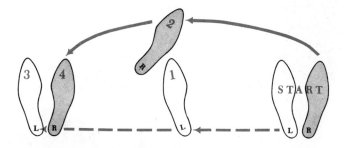

START

1. Step to left side with left foot (slow).
2. Cross right foot in front of left (slow).
3. Step to left side with left foot (quick).
4. Bring right foot next to left (quick).

Dancing the Conversation Step with a Partner. The man retains his right-arm hold for the entire step, but during counts one and two (slow, slow) he opens position slightly with his left hand. Thus, as he steps Side Left and Cross Right, he and his partner are almost side by side — his right side next to her left. He closes position again on counts three and four (quick, quick). Turn to pages 68 and 69 to see illustrations.

The Conversation Step can also be danced in more open position — with the man dropping hold entirely with his left hand.

GIRL'S PART when a man leads the Conversation Step

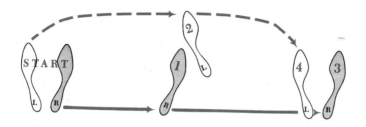

START

1. Step to right side with right foot (slow).
2. Cross left foot over and in front of right (slow).
3. Step to right side with right foot (quick).
4. Bring left foot next to right, weight on left (quick).

First read all instructions for the man's part of the Conversation Step on the opposite page. This will make it easier for you to understand your own part.

Imagine that a man is leading you while you practice this pattern.

If you have any difficulty in learning the Conversation Step, stop in at your nearest Arthur Murray Studio for a personal demonstration.

THE CONVERSATION STEP—OPEN POSITION

When dancing with a partner, the Conversation Step may be done in a half-open position as illustrated above. This step allows partners to talk and dance easily.

How to Use the Conversation Step in the Line of Direction

REVIEW "How to Progress Around a Dance Floor" on page 19. This describes and illustrates the correct Line of Direction in which to proceed while dancing.

Although the Conversation Step moves *sideward,* it must also adhere to the general counterclockwise circling of the dance floor. Thus, in the Conversation Step or any other sideward pattern, the man's left hand (which is holding the girl's right hand) should *point toward the Line of Direction.*

To lead a girl into the Conversation Step, the man should precede it with a pattern that will turn him one quarter to his right. For example, he can use the first half of the Senior Walk, page 58. That is merely a Forward Magic Step turning right on the second slow count. The man will then be pointing with his left hand toward the Line of Direction, in perfect position to start as many repetitions of the Conversation Step as he chooses.

After repeating the Conversation Step a few times, the man can use any pattern that will turn him one quarter to his left. For example, he can use the second half of the Senior Walk or a Magic Left Turn. He will then again be facing the Line of Direction.

What Is Meant by Follow-Through in Dancing

"FOLLOW-THROUGH" is a term that is used to describe the smoothness needed for many muscular accomplishments. In golf or tennis, a player must follow through to make his swing become an even, smooth stroke through the air. Only then will he be able to hit the ball straight toward the goal. A skater must follow through before he can perform the perfected, smooth curves of a figure eight.

In dancing also, follow-through is used to describe smoothness — which is the main requisite of graceful action.

How to Achieve Correct Follow-Through

1. Always keep your feet in a close parallel line when walking forward or back. Note in the Forward Magic Step, page 54, that footsteps 1 and 2 move ahead in a straight line. In the Magic Step Backward, page 56, footsteps 1 and 2 move back in a similarly straight line.
2. Always bring your feet together before stepping to the side. You will find a basic example of this in the same Magic Steps mentioned above. Note that footprint 3, which steps to the side, is not placed directly sideward. It curves toward and past footprint 2.

For practice, review your Magic Steps and exaggerate the follow-through by letting your third step actually brush against your other foot before completing the step to the side.

The Conversation Pivot

THE CONVERSATION PIVOT includes the first two counts of the Conversation Step, which you have already learned, plus basic pivot action. A pivot is a sharp turn taken on one foot.

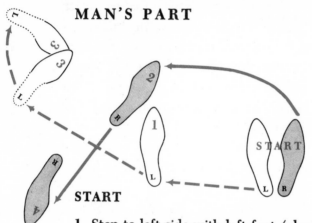

MAN'S PART

1. Step to left side with left foot (slow).
2. Cross right foot over and in front of left, in Conversation position (slow).
3. Step back on left foot, *pivoting right on toes of left foot* (quick).
4. Step forward on right foot, pivoting right with full weight on right (quick).

When you step back on your left foot, to start pivoting, bring the girl to regular closed dancing position. Use that closed position for both pivoting steps (quick, quick).

On the two quick, pivoting steps, you should complete a half turn. By repeating the entire pattern, you will thus execute a full turn and will again face the Line of Direction.

Note that the Conversation Pivot ends with feet apart. *Be sure to follow through with your left foot before you repeat the pattern or start another.*

GIRL'S PART when a man leads
the Conversation Pivot

Reminder: Always study the man's part of a step pattern before learning your own part. Then, as you practice, you can more readily imagine how to dance the step in partnership position.

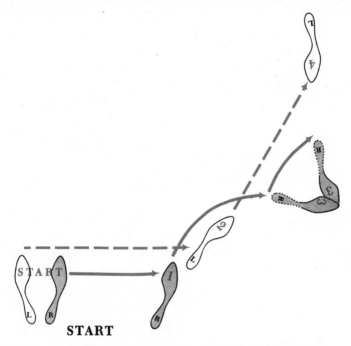

START

1. Step to right side with right foot (slow).
2. Cross left foot over and in front of right, in Conversation position (slow).
3. Step forward on right foot, pivoting *right* on the sole of your right foot (quick).
4. Step back on left foot, pivoting *right*, weight on toes of left foot (quick).

Follow through with right foot as you repeat the Conversation Pivot or start a new pattern.

The Magic Right Turn

THE MAGIC RIGHT TURN is a very useful step on a crowded floor. Although it is harder for a man to turn right than left, this pattern is well worth practice! Count: Slow, slow, quick, quick.

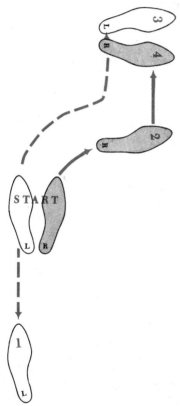

MAN'S PART

START

1. Step back with left foot (slow).
2. Step forward with right foot, turning right (slow).
3. Step to left side with left foot (quick).
4. Bring right foot next to left, weight on right (quick).

By repeating the Magic Right Turn three or four times, you can gracefully maneuver around a corner and regain the Line of Direction.

Should you want to see a complimentary demonstration of this step by expert dancers, stop in at your nearest Arthur Murray studio. You will be cordially welcomed.

GIRL'S PART when a man leads the Magic Right Turn

START

1. Step forward with right foot (slow).
2. Step back with left foot, turning right (slow).
3. Step to right side with right foot (quick).
4. Bring left foot next to right, weight on left (quick).

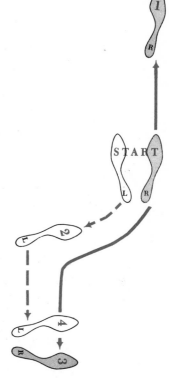

The Magic Turns are good exercise patterns in learning to shift your weight readily forward, back and to the side. After you have studied the man's part and learned your own part of the pattern, do not repeat the step continuously more than three or four times. Stop then and start again to avoid dizziness.

Count: Slow, slow, quick, quick.

The Forward Magic Rhythm

ONE OF the most graceful variations of the Magic Step is the Forward Magic Rhythm because it allows dancers to move rapidly and gracefully around the room in the Line of Direction.

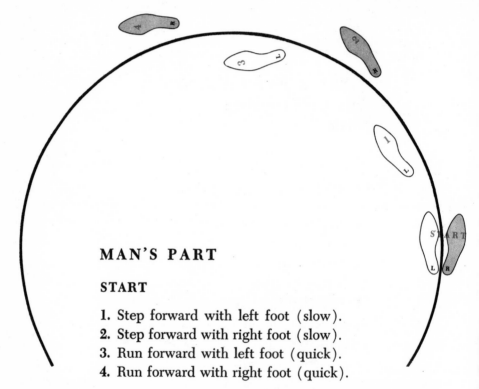

MAN'S PART

START

1. Step forward with left foot (slow).
2. Step forward with right foot (slow).
3. Run forward with left foot (quick).
4. Run forward with right foot (quick).

That's all. Just two long, slow steps, and two short, quick steps but all four steps in the Forward Magic Rhythm should be done very smoothly. Count: Slow, slow, quick, quick.

Be sure that you do not let your heels touch the floor when doing the last two quick steps.

The Forward Magic Rhythm is one of the most useful dance steps for weaving in and out on a crowded floor.

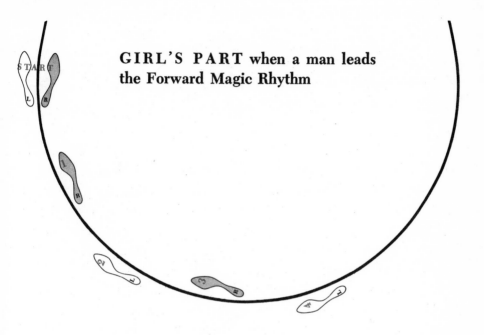

GIRL'S PART when a man leads
the Forward Magic Rhythm

START

1. Step far back with right foot (slow).
2. Step far back with left foot (slow).
3. Run back with right foot (quick).
4. Run back with left foot (quick).

The Magic Rhythm pattern helps to teach a girl lightness. This step, in itself, is an exceptionally good practice exercise for a girl, since it combines backward walking and running steps.

Be sure to practice the pattern with your toes leading during your backward walks and runs. Practice in the Line of Direction, which, when you dance backward, means that your left hand is nearer the wall.

A Simple Fox Trot Routine

HAVE YOU ever noticed a good swimmer who is thoroughly at ease in the water? He dives in, may swim the crawl for a while, turn over on his back and float, and then continue with the trudgen or breast stroke. Perhaps he treads water or swims lazily on his back. He varies the strokes at his command as the mood seizes him.

So it is with a good dancer. Master of the basic steps and their variations, he weaves his own patterns around the dance floor, guided by the mood of the music or his own whim. His dancing is interesting to his partner and to himself.

Therefore, when I give you simple Fox Trot routines, as I do here, remember these are just suggested ways to combine the steps you have learned. Make your own combinations. Only when your dancing becomes your own original creation will you experience the full pleasure of expressing yourself in rhythm.

I am giving you these practice routines for two reasons:

1. They will serve as a review of the steps you have learned. Pay special attention to the changes from one step to another. Practice until you can go from one step into the next smoothly, without halting and with graceful follow-through of footwork. Remember, each pattern starts with the LEFT foot for the man, and the RIGHT foot for the girl.
2. By practicing a series of steps, you will learn to maneuver around the floor in the correct Line of Direction.

Practice Combinations in Fox Trot

EACH OF THE FOLLOWING combinations includes three step patterns. Repeat each step pattern twice in succession.

Practice the combinations in the Line of Direction. Then, after perfecting these samples of step pattern routines, try combinations of your own.

COMBINATION A
MAGIC STEP FORWARD
SENIOR WALK
MAGIC LEFT TURN

COMBINATION B
MAGIC STEP FORWARD*
CONVERSATION STEP
JUNIOR WALK

COMBINATION C
MAGIC STEP FORWARD*
CONVERSATION PIVOT
MAGIC RIGHT TURN

COMBINATION D
MAGIC STEP FORWARD*
THREE CHASSÉS WITH MAGIC LEFT TURN
FORWARD MAGIC RHYTHM

* In B, C and D, the Magic Step Forward is followed by a sideward pattern. Sideward patterns should be taken pointing toward the Line of Direction. Therefore, on the Final Repetition of Magic Step Forward, turn one quarter to your right on the second slow count.

The Curve of Learning

COLLEGE PROFESSORS have a useful phrase to describe the way most students learn. They call it the Curve of Learning. If the progress made by the average pupil was drawn on paper, it would look somewhat like this:

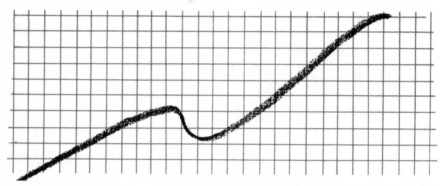

Note that the first part of the line makes an abrupt rise. That shows the speed at which the average pupil learns when he begins studying a new subject. His progress is rapid; his confidence mounts and he is anxious to rush ahead.

Then there is *always* a period of discouragement. You may have reached that point now. Perhaps you may be having difficulty in practicing your steps in a series, with music. Perhaps you may feel that you *cannot* remember without referring to the printed pages of instruction.

Should you have reached your period of discouragement, you must realize that this happens to everyone. Be reassured. Every normal person is born with the ability to move rhythmically. You *can* learn to dance. Give yourself time.

Besides, after a dip in the Curve of Learning, the average student progresses steadily ahead toward his goal!

Part Three

THE WALTZ
AND ITS VARIATIONS

The Waltz

FEW MODERN dances can boast of a background so rich in tradition as the Waltz. Originating in Italy four centuries ago as a round dance called the *Volte,* it has passed through many stages. Each succeeding decade has added something to its charm — until today it is recognized as one of the most beautiful dances in the world.

Most of the Waltz melodies are dreamy and romantic. The steps are smooth and gliding — the pattern of the dance is gay and joyful. And because the Waltz steps are the basic foundation for many other dances, you should really learn to Waltz well.

Waltz Rhythm

THERE ARE *three* beats to each measure of Waltz music, and the music itself plainly suggests that you count:

ONE, two, three ... ONE, two, three ...

This same beat is carried through the entire Waltz, and therefore it is very easy to keep time once you have learned the steps.

Naturally, in every Waltz song there are both long notes and short notes; frequently one note lasts three beats, as in the familiar "Sidewalks of New York" ("East Side, West Side, All Around the Town"), in which each of the first four notes is given three beats:

EAST	SIDE,	WEST	SIDE
1-2-3	1-2-3	1-2-3	1-2-3

If you will hum "ONE, two, three — ONE, two, three" instead

of "East Side, etc.," to this well-known tune, I am sure you will quickly grasp its Waltz rhythm without a bit of difficulty.

Accent in the Waltz

AN IMPORTANT KEY to a colorful dancing personality is *accent*. It is just as essential in dancing as in music or in speaking. A person who talks with a flat, unvarying voice and a "deadpan" expression is sure to sound like a bore.

A dancer who does not accent and vary his dancing isn't much fun as a partner. His leading has no life or pep. And by the same token, the girl who hasn't learned to dance alone — with a full knowledge of the man's part of each step — usually has little life to her dancing. She doesn't know how or when to accent the beat and rhythm of the dance — to express that extra something that makes dancing with her a real joy.

Dancers should emphasize, or accent, the same beat of music that the orchestra accents most. As I told you in a previous chapter, observe (or listen to, on the radio or phonograph) the accented beats of the bass drummer. When he is playing a Waltz, for example, he strikes the pedal of his drum in groups of three beats, but he strikes hardest on the first beat.

Therefore, when you practice the Waltz, you should do the same — accent the *first* of every three steps.

And remember: Accent or emphasis is marked by the man's left foot, and the girl's right foot.

Try this way of injecting more life and pep into your dancing, and after only a few hours of practice you will find yourself accenting the correct beats quite naturally.

The Basic Waltz Step

THE BASIC WALTZ STEP is composed of three simple counts. It is one of the most useful dance steps — you will find the pattern in both Waltz and Fox Trot turns and in almost every simple and advanced Waltz step.

MAN'S PART

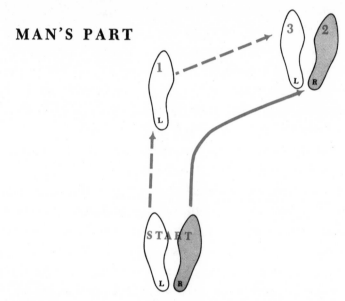

START

1. Step directly forward with your left foot.
2. Step diagonally forward with your right foot.
3. Bring your left foot next to your right, weight on left.

Remember to follow through on the second step. While practicing, exaggerate this by actually brushing your right foot against the left before placing it diagonally forward.

Accent your first step.

GIRL'S PART when a man leads the Basic Waltz Step

BE SURE to study and learn the man's part. When you reach the Box Step in the Waltz, you will be using exactly that pattern.

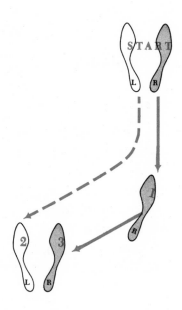

START

1. Step back on your right foot.
2. Step diagonally back on your left foot.
3. Bring your right foot next to your left, weight on right.

As mentioned in the instructions for the man, be sure to follow through on your second step. Also, accent count 1.

The Forward Waltz Step

THE COMPLETE Forward Waltz Step takes two measures or six counts. The first three counts are the Basic Waltz, which you have already learned. Now add three more counts which will repeat a similar pattern starting with the alternate foot.

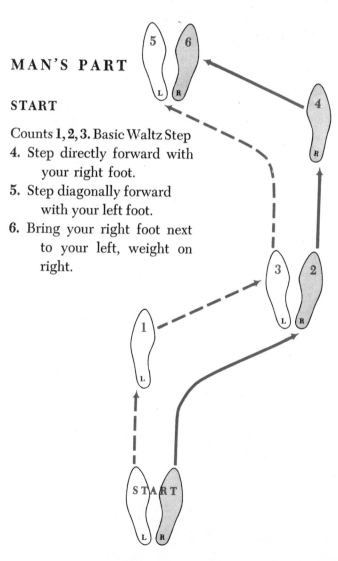

MAN'S PART

START

Counts 1, 2, 3. Basic Waltz Step
4. Step directly forward with your right foot.
5. Step diagonally forward with your left foot.
6. Bring your right foot next to your left, weight on right.

GIRL'S PART when a man leads
the Forward Waltz Step

FIRST PRACTICE the man's part. Since it is easier to Waltz forward, you will be able to concentrate on perfecting your footwork. Keep your feet in a straight line on counts 1 and 4. Remember to follow through on counts 2 and 5. *Emphasize the follow-through.*

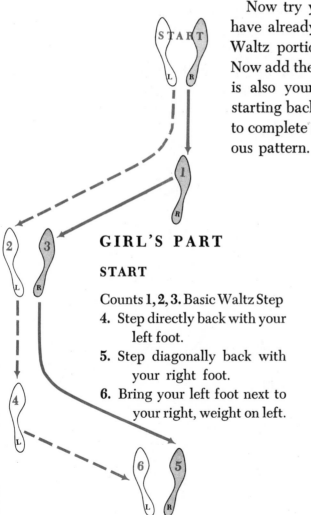

Now try your own part. You have already learned the Basic Waltz portion of three counts. Now add the new portion which is also your Basic Waltz, but starting back with your *left* foot to complete a six-count continuous pattern.

GIRL'S PART

START

Counts 1, 2, 3. Basic Waltz Step
4. Step directly back with your left foot.
5. Step diagonally back with your right foot.
6. Bring your left foot next to your right, weight on left.

The Backward Waltz Step

To WALTZ WELL, you must be able to dance forward and back and to turn in either direction. If you have followed the preceding instructions, you have already learned to Waltz forward. Next you must learn to Waltz backward. Once you have accomplished this, your basic, progressive Waltz patterns can be linked together with turns, thus offering a variety of flowing movements.

The backward Waltz Step is just the opposite of the same pattern taken forward but it requires special study. Give yourself ample practice. Accent counts 1 and 4. Use follow-through footwork on counts 2 and 5.

MAN'S PART

START

1. Step directly back with left foot.
2. Step diagonally back with right foot.
3. Bring left foot next to right, weight on left.
4. Step straight back with right foot.
5. Step diagonally back with left foot.
6. Bring right foot next to left, weight on right.

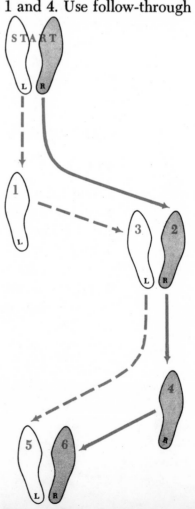

GIRL'S PART when a man leads
the Backward Waltz Step

NOTE that when a man leads his Backward Waltz Step, you will be dancing forward. I suggested, in the preceding lesson, that you learn the man's part of the Forward Waltz. If you did master it, review the pattern now, by imagining yourself following a partner.

Continue concentrating on accent and follow-through. I emphasize these reminders because they are essential to good dancing.

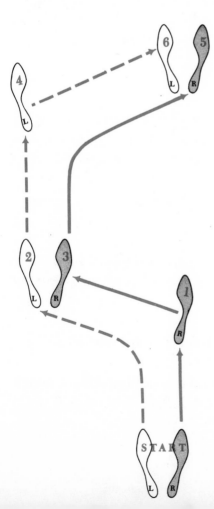

GIRL'S PART

START

1. Step directly *forward* with *right* foot.
2. Step diagonally forward with left foot.
3. Bring right foot next to left, weight on right.
4. Step directly *forward* with *left* foot.
5. Step diagonally forward with right foot.
6. Bring left foot next to right, weight on left.

The Senior Waltz

THE SENIOR WALTZ combines the Forward Waltz of six counts with the Backward Waltz, also of six counts. But a quarter turn is added to each of these Waltz patterns. Review "Which is a Right Turn, and Which is a Left?" on page 33.

It will be easier for you to learn the Senior Waltz by dividing the full pattern into its two separate portions.

MAN'S PART

First Portion: Glance back at your part of the Forward Waltz Step, page 86. Dance the Forward Waltz, *but turning one quarter to your right on count 4.*

For practice, repeat several times without music; then repeat for a full record of music.

Second Portion: Now look at your part of the Backward Waltz Step, page 88. Dance it, *turning one quarter to your left on count 4.*

You will need extra practice for the backward portion.

Now, combine the first and second portions alternately. Count in measures: 1, 2, 3 (turn) 4, 5, 6; 1, 2, 3 (turn) 4, 5, 6.

GIRL'S PART when a man leads
the Senior Waltz

PLEASE READ the entire facing page of instructions for the man's part of the Senior Waltz.

Before attempting your own part, try the man's part of the Senior Waltz, exactly as given — in two separate portions and then the combination of these portions. Only after you have mastered the man's instructions for the entire Senior Waltz pattern should you learn your own part.

GIRL'S PART

First Portion: Look at page 87, which gives your part *when the man leads the Forward Waltz*. Note that you will be going *backward*. Dance this portion *turning one quarter to your right on count 4*. Practice thoroughly.

Second Portion: Now see page 89, which gives your part *when the man leads the Backward Waltz*. Note that you will be dancing *forward*. Try this portion *turning one quarter to your left on count 4*.

Combine the two portions of your own part. Practice until you can turn smoothly and lightly.

The Box Step

I HAVE never forgotten what a well-known author once said to me: "I took dancing lessons as a child, but I got discouraged — I could never get out of the box!"

The Box Step is merely a combination of the Basic Waltz forward and back, so it is really not difficult. But it takes practice to master the changes of weight that coincide with the back-and-forth directions. However, the Box Step is well worth the time it may take you to learn thoroughly, for it has many uses. *It is the basis for turning left and right in the Waltz;* it is also a foundation pattern in Rumba, Mambo and Samba.

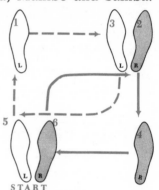

MAN'S PART

START

1. Step directly forward with left foot. (Accent this count.)
2. Step to the right side with your right foot. (Follow through!)
3. Bring left foot next to right, weight on left.
4. Step straight *back* with right foot. (Accent this count.)
5. Step to your left side with left foot. (Follow through!)
6. Bring right foot next to left, weight on right.

GIRL'S PART when a man leads the Box Step

THE GIRL's PART of the Box Step is exactly the same as the man's except that she does the Basic Waltz back and then forward, while the man dances forward and then back.

Pay special attention to your follow-through footwork.

GIRL'S PART

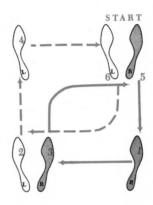

START

1. Step directly back with right foot. (Accent this count.)
2. Step to the left side with your left foot. (Follow through.)
3. Bring right foot next to left, weight on right.
4. Step directly *forward* with left foot. (Accent this count.)
5. Step to your right side with right foot. (Follow through.)
6. Bring left foot next to right, weight on left.

The Left Waltz Turn

First study the instructions, then the diagram. Note that the Left Waltz Turn is merely a turning adaptation of the Box Step.

This is a turn that you will rely on once you start dancing with a variety of partners. Therefore, make up your mind to learn the Left Waltz Turn perfectly! Should you have any difficulty understanding the instructions, *review the Box Step.*

MAN'S PART

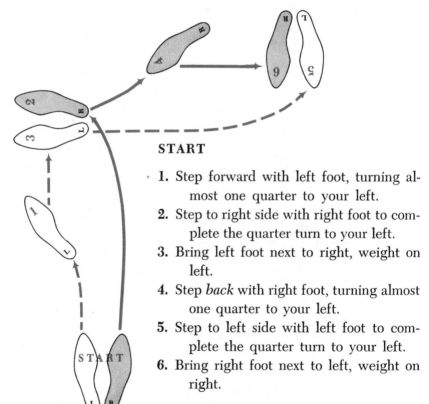

START

1. Step forward with left foot, turning almost one quarter to your left.
2. Step to right side with right foot to complete the quarter turn to your left.
3. Bring left foot next to right, weight on left.
4. Step *back* with right foot, turning almost one quarter to your left.
5. Step to left side with left foot to complete the quarter turn to your left.
6. Bring right foot next to left, weight on right.

You must realize that this pattern completes a half turn. By repeating the entire six-count step, you will again be facing the Line of Direction.

GIRL'S PART when a man leads the Left Waltz Turn

In TURNING patterns, it is absolutely essential that you understand the man's part. Therefore, study the facing page thoroughly.

GIRL'S PART

START

1. Step back with right foot, turning almost one quarter to your left.
2. Step to left side with left foot to complete the quarter turn to your left.
3. Bring right foot next to left, weight on right.
4. Step *forward* with left foot, turning almost one quarter to your left.
5. Step to right side with right foot to complete the quarter turn to your left.
6. Bring left foot next to right, weight on left.

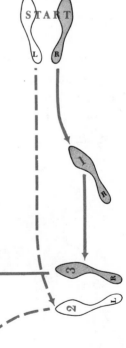

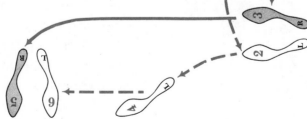

Balance Steps in the Waltz

A BALANCE STEP may be taken in any of the four directions — forward, backward, or to your left or right side.

When you take a Balance Step in the Waltz, you step on the count of one and *hold your weight on that foot for two additional counts.* The other foot is brought slowly in place *but with no weight on it.*

This same description applies whether you are balancing forward, back or to either side while waltzing.

As a man balances forward, the girl balances back. When he balances back, she goes forward. A man's balance to the left would lead the girl to balance to her right, etc. *Therefore, these two pages of instructions are for man and girl.*

Balancing Forward. Practice Pattern.

Counts **1, 2, 3.** Step forward with left foot and balance weight on that foot for two more counts as you slowly draw right foot next to left, *no weight on right.*
Counts **4, 5, 6.** Step forward with right foot and balance weight on that foot for two more counts as you slowly draw left foot next to right, *no weight on left.*
Repeat continuously in the Line of Direction around the room.

Balancing Backward

AFTER YOU HAVE mastered the forward Balances described on the facing page, practice the same movements progressing *backward*.

This illustration shows the man balancing on his left foot and bringing his right foot back, without weight on it. Counts **1, 2, 3**. Step back with left foot and balance weight on that foot for two more counts as you slowly draw right foot next to left. *No weight on right.* Counts **4, 5, 6**. Step back with right foot and balance weight on that foot for two more counts as you slowly draw left foot next to right. *No weight on left.*

BALANCE STEP TO LEFT SIDE

Take a long step with left foot directly to left side; hold weight on left for two additional beats. (As you draw right foot up to left, no weight on right.)

BALANCE STEP TO RIGHT SIDE

Step to right side with right foot and balance weight on this foot for two additional beats of waltz music. (As you draw left foot up to right, no weight on left.)

The Biltmore

THIS IS A favorite pattern of all good dancers. It can be done forward or back and consists of a Balance Step of three counts plus a Basic Waltz. Reminder! *A dotted footprint signifies that there is no weight placed on that step.*

MAN'S PART

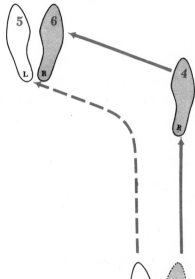

START

1, 2, 3. Step forward with left foot *and balance weight on that foot for two more counts* as you slowly bring right foot next to left. No weight on right.

4, 5, 6. Basic Waltz Forward starting with *right* foot. Accent count 4.

After mastering the Biltmore, practice it in successive repetition around the room in the Line of Direction.

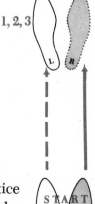

GIRL'S PART when a man leads
the Biltmore, Forward

THE BILTMORE is not only an effective step in appearance but it is particularly useful as a practice pattern for a girl. The Balance portion, followed by a Basic Waltz, will teach you to be alert and light to lead.

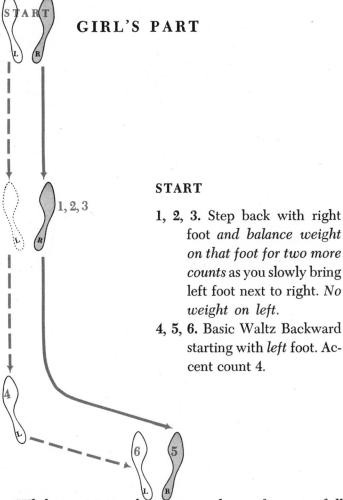

GIRL'S PART

START

1, 2, 3. Step back with right foot *and balance weight on that foot for two more counts* as you slowly bring left foot next to right. *No weight on left.*

4, 5, 6. Basic Waltz Backward starting with *left* foot. Accent count 4.

While practicing this pattern, do not forget to follow through with footstep 5.

The Biltmore, Backward

ALTHOUGH the Biltmore done backward is just the reverse of the forward pattern, it will take practice to achieve. To dance backward is always harder for a man to master.

MAN'S PART

START

1, 2, 3. Step *back* with left foot *and balance weight on that foot for two more counts* as you slowly bring right foot next to left. No weight on right.

4, 5, 6. Basic Waltz Backward starting with *right* foot. Accent count 4. Follow through on count 5.

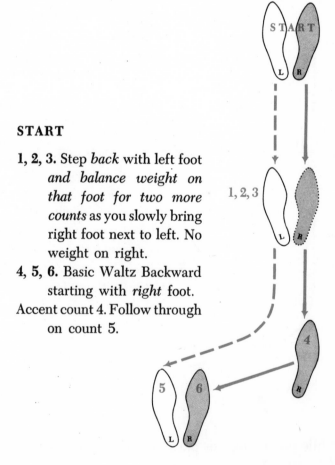

GIRL'S PART when a man leads
The Biltmore, Backward

IN THIS PATTERN you will have an opportunity to practice a Balance forward. Do not be afraid to take a long step forward — the man will be stepping back, out of your way. *A short forward step makes a girl seem heavy as a partner.*

GIRL'S PART

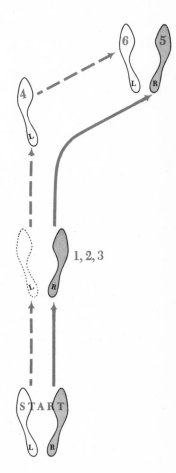

START

1, 2, 3. Step *forward* with right foot *and balance weight on that foot for two more counts* as you slowly bring left foot next to right. *No weight on left.*

4, 5, 6. Basic Waltz Forward, starting with *left* foot.

The Hesitation

THE HESITATION is universally popular. Like the Biltmore, it is a combination of a Balance with a Basic Waltz, but since the Waltz portion is done turning, the Hesitation is a more advanced, effective pattern.

Read the instructions and study the diagram before trying the step. It is always easier to concentrate on turns when you have memorized the pattern and do not have to hold the book in your hand.

MAN'S PART

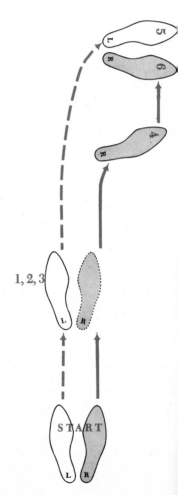

START

1, 2, 3. Step forward with left foot and balance weight on that foot for two more counts as you slowly bring right foot next to left. *No weight on right.*

4. Step forward with right foot, turning almost one quarter to your right.

5. Step to left side with left foot, completing the quarter turn to your right.

6. Bring right foot next to left, weight on right.

GIRL'S PART when a man leads the Hesitation

ANY PATTERN that includes a Balance Step is an exacting test of a girl's ability to follow lightly. Since the Hesitation combines a Balance with a turn, it will furnish you with an excellent opportunity for practice.

Review page 33 to be sure of your direction in turning.

GIRL'S PART

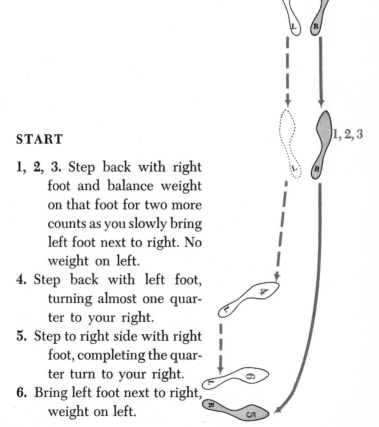

START

1, 2, 3. Step back with right foot and balance weight on that foot for two more counts as you slowly bring left foot next to right. No weight on left.

4. Step back with left foot, turning almost one quarter to your right.

5. Step to right side with right foot, completing the quarter turn to your right.

6. Bring left foot next to right, weight on left.

The Hesitation, Backward

You will find the Hesitation, done backward, to be a very useful step at the corner of a room. It is the direct opposite of the Hesitation done forward but will take practice to achieve smoothly.

MAN'S PART

START

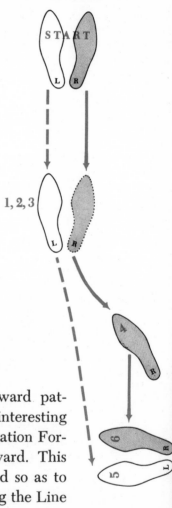

1, 2, 3. Step *back* with left foot *and balance weight on that foot for two more counts* as you slowly bring right foot next to left. *No weight on right.*
4. Step back with right foot, turning almost one quarter to your left.
5. Step to left side with left foot, completing the quarter turn to your left.
6. Bring right foot next to left, weight on right.

After mastering this backward pattern, you can form a very interesting combination alternating Hesitation Forward with Hesitation Backward. This combination should be danced so as to progress in a zigzag path along the Line of Direction.

GIRL'S PART when a man leads
The Hesitation, Backward

HERE AGAIN is a Waltz pattern in which you will start *forward*. Take that step confidently, weight held forward and on the ball of your foot.

Imagine that a man is leading you as you practice. Hold your arms in partnership position.

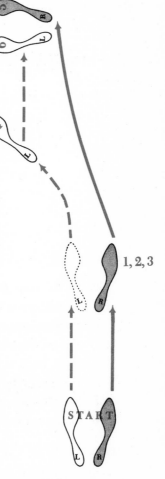

GIRL'S PART

START

1, 2, 3. Step *forward* with right foot *and balance weight on that foot for two more counts* as you slowly bring left foot next to right. *No weight on left.*

4. Step *forward* with left foot, turning almost one quarter to your left.

5. Step to right side with right foot, completing the quarter turn to your left.

6. Bring left foot next to right, weight on left.

Continue accenting the first count of every Waltz measure — in this pattern, counts 1 and 4.

The Arthur Murray Turn

HERE IS another variation of a Waltz turn that combines a balance with a Basic Waltz. This is one of my favorite patterns because it is effective-looking and easy to lead on a crowded floor.

Remember that you put no weight on a dotted footprint.

MAN'S PART

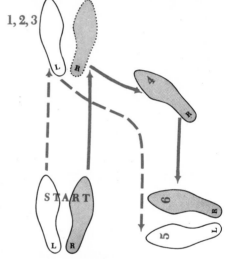

START

1, 2, 3. Step forward with left foot and hold your weight on that foot for two more counts as you slowly bring right foot next to left. No weight on right.
4. Step back with *right* foot, turning one quarter to your left.
5. Step to left side with left foot.
6. Bring right foot next to left.

After perfecting this pattern, practice it turning a bit more than a quarter turn to your left on the Basic Waltz portion. Then, by repeating the entire step three times, you will be able to make a complete turn to again face the Line of Direction.

GIRL'S PART when a man leads
the Arthur Murray Turn

READ the entire facing page and then try the man's part. Practice it until you can dance it repeatedly to music.

Then study your own part, which starts with a balance back on your right foot.

GIRL'S PART

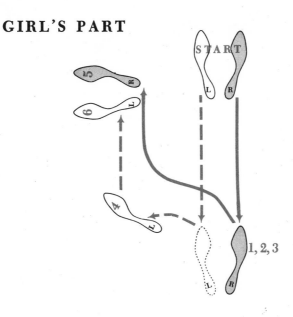

START

1, 2, 3. Step back with right foot and hold your weight on that foot for two more counts as you slowly bring left foot next to right. No weight on left.

4. Step forward with left foot, turning one quarter to your left.

5. Step to right side with right foot.

6. Bring left foot next to right.

The Yale Waltz

HERE IS a combination of Basic Waltz with a balance to the side. This, like the preceding step, is especially useful in avoiding other couples on a crowded dance floor.

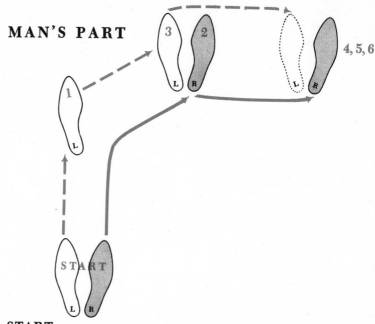

MAN'S PART

START

1. Step forward with left foot.
2. Step diagonally forward with right foot.
3. Bring left foot next to right.
4, 5, 6. Step to right side with right foot and hold weight on that foot for two more counts as you slowly bring left foot next to right. No weight on left.

Continue concentrating on good style as you practice. *Take a long step on count 1, accenting it. Follow through with count 2.*

GIRL'S PART when a man leads the Yale Waltz

IT WILL BE particularly useful for you to learn the man's part of the Yale Waltz, because it will give you the opportunity of practicing a balance to the right side.

Then when you study your own part, you will also learn to balance to the left.

GIRL'S PART

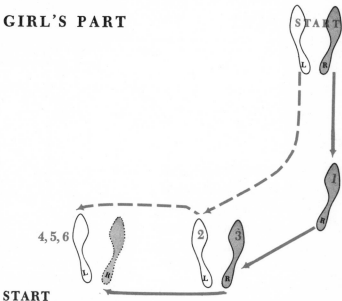

START

1. Step back with right foot.
2. Step diagonally back with left foot.
3. Bring right foot next to left.
4, 5, 6. Step to left side with left foot and hold weight on that foot for two more counts as you slowly bring right foot next to left. No weight on right.

REMINDER: When you take a backward step, make it a long one, stretching from the ankle and reaching with the toes.

The Kathryn Murray Turn

THIS IS A good pattern to use at the corner of a room. With successive repetition, you will be able to make a whole turn within very little space and again be ready to start forward in the Line of Direction.

MAN'S PART

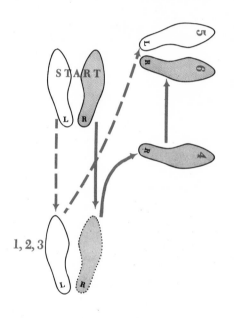

START

1, 2, 3. Step directly back with left foot and hold weight on that foot for two more counts as you slowly bring right foot back, next to left. No weight on right.

4. Step forward with right foot, turning one quarter to your right.

5. Step to left side with left foot.

6. Bring right foot next to left.

After sufficient practice, you will be able to turn a bit more than one quarter to your right on the Basic Waltz portion. When you have reached that advanced ability, you will be able to make a complete turn quite easily by repeating this entire pattern three times.

GIRL'S PART when a man leads
the Kathryn Murray Turn

SOME YEARS ago when I asked my wife what she would like as a birthday celebration, she said, "Name a popular step for me." So I chose this Waltz turn that she particularly liked. I think you will enjoy it, too.

Continue learning the man's part first so that you will have a better visual image of your own part.

GIRL'S PART

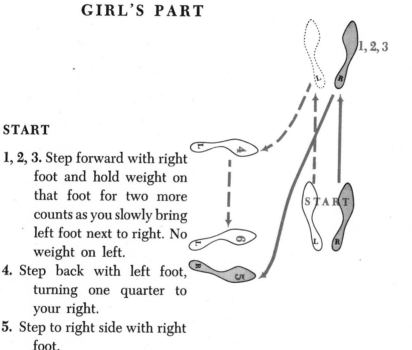

START

1, 2, 3. Step forward with right foot and hold weight on that foot for two more counts as you slowly bring left foot next to right. No weight on left.

4. Step back with left foot, turning one quarter to your right.

5. Step to right side with right foot.

6. Bring left foot next to right.

The Right Waltz Turn

BEFORE you start studying the Right Waltz Turn, it is essential that you remember this one standard rule of ballroom dancing: A man always starts a pattern with his *left* foot.

Since the Right Waltz Turn starts with a man's *right* foot, it is obvious that some other pattern must precede it.

Also, a pattern must end with the man's weight on his *right* foot so that he can either repeat or start a new pattern according to standard rule. But the Right Waltz Turn finishes with the man's weight on his *left* foot. Therefore some other ending must be added.

So, when you learn the Right Waltz Turn, described on the facing page, please realize that *it is always used as a portion of a sequence of step patterns*. After you have mastered the turn you will find directions for using it in partnership dancing.

The Right Waltz Turn is a turning adaptation of the Box Step. Review page 92.

MAN'S PART of the
Right Waltz Turn

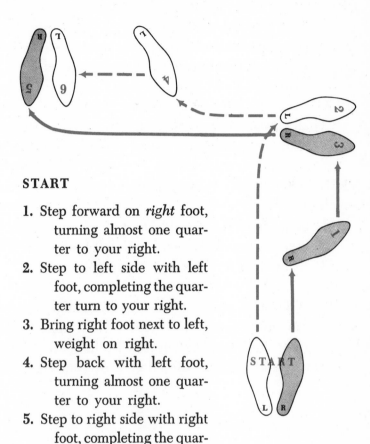

START

1. Step forward on *right* foot, turning almost one quarter to your right.
2. Step to left side with left foot, completing the quarter turn to your right.
3. Bring right foot next to left, weight on right.
4. Step back with left foot, turning almost one quarter to your right.
5. Step to right side with right foot, completing the quarter turn to your right.
6. Bring left foot next to right, weight on left.

PRACTICE the Right Waltz Turn until you can dance it easily in time to music. Then read the next page, which gives instructions for using the turn in a sequence of step patterns.

How to Use a Right Waltz Turn Within a Sequence of Step Patterns

FIRST PORTION: Basic Waltz Forward.
1. Step forward with left foot.
2. Step diagonally forward with right foot.
3. Bring left foot next to right, weight on left.

SECOND PORTION: Right Waltz Turn.
Then *repeat the turn*, so that you will again be facing the Line of Direction. With the repeat, this totals twelve counts.

THIRD PORTION: Basic Waltz Forward, starting with right foot.
1. Step forward with right foot.
2. Step diagonally forward with left foot.
3. Bring right foot next to left, weight on right.

PRACTICE these patterns until you can dance the entire sequence smoothly, easily and without faltering. After you can keep perfect time, imagine yourself leading a partner. Visualize how you would indicate direction with your right hand.

GIRL'S PART when a man leads the Right Waltz Turn

START

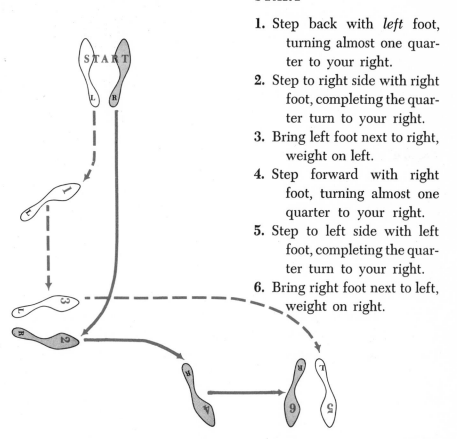

1. Step back with *left* foot, turning almost one quarter to your right.
2. Step to right side with right foot, completing the quarter turn to your right.
3. Bring left foot next to right, weight on left.
4. Step forward with right foot, turning almost one quarter to your right.
5. Step to left side with left foot, completing the quarter turn to your right.
6. Bring right foot next to left, weight on right.

Study the above six-count turn until you can try it without holding the book in your hand.

Then practice the turn thoroughly. When you are completely sure that you can dance it easily in time to music, read the facing page, which describes a sequence of step patterns.

Your own part of the sequence will be the direct opposite of the man's instructions. You will use a Basic Waltz Backward starting with the right foot for the first portion and a Basic Waltz Backward starting with the *left* foot for the third portion.

Practice Combinations of Waltz Patterns

PLEASE REMEMBER that when I give you practice routines of steps, they are for *practice* only so that you will become accustomed to moving around a floor in the Line of Direction.

Once you have had sufficient dancing experience, the various step patterns you have learned will be automatically at your command. You will not need any set routine — you will dance as the music prompts you.

COMBINATION A

TWELVE COUNTS OF SENIOR WALTZ
TWELVE COUNTS OF LEFT WALTZ TURN

COMBINATION B

TWELVE COUNTS COMBINING FORWARD HESITATION (SIX COUNTS) WITH BACK HESITATION (SIX COUNTS).
DANCE THIS IN A ZIGZAG PATH AROUND THE FLOOR, IN THE LINE OF DIRECTION.

COMBINATION C

TWELVE COUNTS OF YALE BALANCE
TWELVE COUNTS OF KATHRYN MURRAY TURN

COMBINATION D

SIX COUNTS OF FORWARD BILTMORE
SIX COUNTS OF KATHRYN MURRAY TURN
SIX COUNTS OF BACKWARD BILTMORE
SIX COUNTS OF ARTHUR MURRAY TURN

The Five Correct Positions
of the Feet

FOR ANY MAN or girl who wants to be a good dancer, *this is the most important page of the whole book* for you to study thoroughly. I waited until now to give you this instruction because a beginner must concentrate on learning step patterns before he can add correct style to his footsteps.

In all ballroom dancing, *with no exception,* your feet must always be placed in one of the five correct positions. Study each picture carefully; read the directions and then practice the exercises given on the following page.

1 When starting to dance, or when the step brings your feet together, this is the correct position for them.

2 When your feet are apart, the toes are always turned out and your weight should rest on one foot only.

3 In bringing your feet together again, you may vary the position shown in the first picture by placing the heel of one foot at the instep of the other.

4 Walking forward or backward should always be in a straight "chalk line"—placing one foot directly in front (or back) of the other.

5 The toes of one foot placed at the heel of the other foot produces this pleasing variation of the position shown in the third picture.

How to Practice the Five Correct Foot Positions

Position One. Stand with feet together, toes turned outward.

Position Two. Practice repeatedly to slow Fox Trot music. Start with feet together in Position One.

1. Keep weight on right foot and point left foot, with toes turned outward, to left side.
2. Return to place in Position One.
3. Keep weight on left foot and point right foot, with toes turned outward, to right side.
4. Return to place in Position One.

Position Three. Repeat the exercise given for Position Two, but on counts 2 and 4, when you bring your foot back to place, do so in Position Three. For example, on count 2 you will bring your left heel to the instep of your right foot. On count 4 you will bring your right heel to the instep of your left foot. Practice to slow Fox Trot music.

Position Four. Review Magic Step Forward and Back, concentrating on keeping your feet in a straight line, toes turned outward, during the walking steps. Continue that straight line by using follow-through before stepping to the side.

Position Five. Repeat the exercise given for Position Two, but on counts 2 and 4, when you bring your foot back to place, do so in Position Five. For example, on count 2 you will bring the toes of your left foot back and at the heel of your right foot. On count 4 you will bring the toes of your right foot back and at the heel of your left foot.

Part Four

THE RUMBA

The Rumba

THE RUMBA, which originated in Cuba, is unique among ballroom dances. The music has a seductive, primitive charm, and yet, when correctly danced, the Rumba is as smooth as the Fox Trot, as decorous as the Waltz.

The *one* essentially different characteristic of the Rumba is the Rumba motion. When you dance the Waltz, the Samba, the Fox Trot, you place your weight on each step that you take. But in the Rumba, *you take each step without placing your weight on that step.*

Once you learn the Rumba motion, your dancing will have a typical Cuban style. The motion is what makes the Rumba different from any other dance. It must be learned and practiced; it cannot be "faked"!

Facts About Rumba

MANY TYPES of Cuban music are called Rumba. But there are more variations of tempo and style in the Rumba than in the Fox Trot. Here is a brief description of some varieties in Rumba tempo.

The very slow Rumbas are called either Bolero, Cancion Bolero or Bolero Son. The last one has a fast ending. The Danzon is of quiet, medium tempo, and the steps that fit the music are conservative in style. Then there is the Danzonette — similar to the Danzon — but the music is shorter and has more life; the Guajero — a slow to medium tempo; the Son Montuno, which is medium with a fast ending; the Guaracha, usually played very fast; and the Montuno, also fast.

The instruments used for Rumba music are distinctive and easy to recognize. The maracas are dried gourds, filled with buckshot. They are shaken like rattles and they add excitement to the music. The bongo is made of two small drums fastened together and held between the knees, drummed upon with the fingers. Finally there are the clavas, which are two pieces of hard wood, about six inches long and about an inch thick. These give a sharp, reverberating sound when struck together.

But a dancer who has mastered a pattern of steps and has practiced them in Rumba style does not have to be concerned with the names of tempos or musical instruments. He can fit his steps to any Rumba music. When he hears the maracas, he can dance with the true confidence that comes with knowledge.

The Secret of the Rumba Motion

IT TOOK ME nine years to discover the secret of the authentic Cuban Rumba. Now that I know it, I can teach it to you in just a few minutes.

In American dances there is no hip movement. But in the Rumba there is a slight rhythmical swaying of the hips. The secret of acquiring this typical Rumba movement is in taking each step with a slightly bent knee. If this is done properly, your hips sway from side to side.

Now here is the trick of getting the Rumba motion. As you take each step with a slightly bent knee, your entire weight remains on the heel of the other foot. For instance, when you step forward with your left foot, your left knee is bent and your weight remains behind on your right foot.

The effect is just the same as walking up a flight of stairs.

The Cuban Walk

START WITH your feet together. Without moving your body forward, take a short step forward with your left foot, bending your left knee . . . and as you bend your left knee, be sure that your entire weight is on the heel of your right foot. Your right foot should be flat on the floor, with your right knee straight.

Now try it with the other foot. Take a short step forward with your right foot. The right knee should be bent, with the weight on the heel of the left foot and the left knee straight. When you bend your knee be sure that you do not stoop. The body should be held erect.

SIDE VIEW

PRACTICE

Start forward now, stepping as described, first left, then right.

If you hold your hands on your hips as you walk, you will notice that your weight shifts from side to side. That is the Rumba motion. That's all there is to it. You don't have to swing your hips or consciously move any other part of your body.

Now practice to the music.

Move forward left — move forward right.

Left, right, left, right.

The Rumba motion will give an authentic Cuban style to your dancing. Learning this motion does take time, but once you master it, you will find the same motion also useful in Mambo, Cha-Cha and Merengue.

FRONT VIEW

Essential Practice of the Cuban Walk

RUMBA MOTION provides the basic styling not only in Rumba, but also for Mambo, Cha-Cha and Merengue. It is impossible to achieve these Latin dances correctly until the undulating hip movement, called Rumba motion, is at your command.

Don't forget that it is natural to place your weight on a step; therefore it takes concentrated practice to learn to walk with the delayed transference of weight that is described on pages 120 through 123. Once you do have control of the motion, you will find it easy to incorporate it while stepping in any direction, to any tempo of music.

So far you have been instructed to use Rumba motion in the Cuban Walk going forward. To test whether you have accomplished this, place your hands on your hips; as you step forward with your left foot, bending the left knee and keeping your weight on your right foot, your *right* hip should be moving slightly outward. As you step forward with your right foot, bending the right knee and keeping your weight on your left foot, your *left* hip should be moving outward.

Continue stepping forward with hands on hips. Use all slow counts, and when the Rumba motion becomes smooth and consistently correct, try it to slow music.

Cuban Walk in Other Directions

To the left side: Step to left side with left foot, bending left knee and keeping weight on right foot.

Bring right foot next to left as you straighten left knee and bend right knee. Weight on left foot.

Repeat successively.

To the right side: Reverse the above description.

Backward: Rumba motion in back steps is more difficult. Allow sufficient time for practice; place hands on hips to test yourself.

REPEATED PRACTICE PATTERN TO MUSIC

All slows, totaling eighteen counts.

Three steps forward — left, right, left.

Three *completed* side steps to right side. (A completed side step takes two counts, since it is side-together. Thus, this portion takes six counts, ending with feet together.)

Three steps back — right, left, right.

Three *completed* side steps to left side (six counts, ending with weight on right foot).

The Cuban Rhythm Step

Now you are ready to adapt your Cuban Walk to the dancing accent of Rumba. Turn on any slow or medium Rumba record and listen to the beat of the music. Count the measures aloud as *slow, quick, quick.*

When you are able to count the beats, practice the Cuban Walk forward, to the sides and backward to the Cuban Rhythm counts of slow, quick, quick.

Continue testing your Rumba motion with hands on hips as described on the facing page. When your hips are undulating smoothly, use the practice pattern described above, *in Cuban Rhythm count.*

The Box Step in the Rumba

IF YOU studied the Waltz section thoroughly, you already know the foot pattern of the Box Step. But to execute the movements with Rumba motion and in time to Rumba music will take special practice.

After reviewing the Box Step itself, add Rumba hip motion. Test yourself by holding your hands on your hips.

MAN'S PART

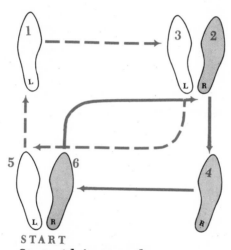

START
Start with feet together.

START

1. Step forward with left foot (slow).
2. Step to right side with right foot (quick).
3. Bring left foot next to right (quick).
4. Step back with right foot (slow).
5. Step to left side with left foot (quick).
6. Bring right foot next to left (quick).

GIRL'S PART when a man leads the Box Step in the Rumba

BEFORE you start your Box Step pattern, be very sure that you have achieved smooth Rumba motion in the Cuban Walk and the Cuban Rhythm step. Study those pages carefully. A girl needs highly perfected and subtle Rumba motion to enhance her dancing appearance.

Until you can move gracefully, with Rumba motion, in each of the four directions, do not attempt the Box Step.

GIRL'S PART

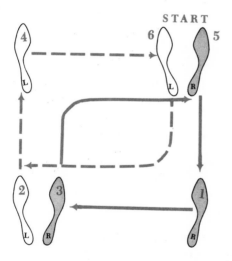

START

1. Step back with right foot (slow).
2. Step to left side with left foot (quick).
3. Bring right foot next to left (quick).
4. Step forward with left foot (slow).
5. Step to right side with right foot (quick).
6. Bring left foot next to right (quick).

The Left Box Turn in the Rumba

ONCE you are thoroughly familiar with the Box Step, learning this turn will be easy. All the steps are exactly the same as in the Box Step.

To do the left turn, you simply do the Box Step, but on the *first* and *fourth* counts turn slightly to your left.

Remember that to turn left you glance over your left shoulder. Here is another helpful hint for leading: A man turning left moves his left hand slightly back.

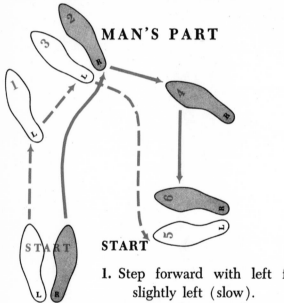

MAN'S PART

START

1. Step forward with left foot, turning slightly left (slow).
2. Step to right side with right foot (quick).
3. Bring left foot next to right (quick).
4. Step back with right foot, turning slightly left (slow).
5. Step to left side with left foot (quick).
6. Bring right foot next to left (quick).

Be sure to use Rumba motion! On every step, move with bent knee, without weight.

GIRL'S PART when a man leads the Left Box Turn in Rumba

I ADVISE that you first try the man's part of the Rumba Box Step. Next, study his part of the Left Box Turn. Imagine yourself leading someone in the Turn so that you can picture how a partner will expect you to respond.

Then study these instructions and this diagram of your own part. Memorize the action so that you can perform the step without holding the book in your hand. Instead, hold your hands on your *hips* to be sure you are including Rumba motion.

GIRL'S PART

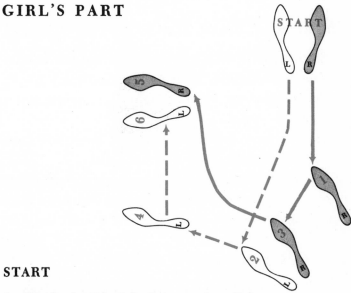

START

1. Step back with right foot, turning slightly left (slow).
2. Step to left side with left foot (quick).
3. Bring right foot next to left (quick).
4. Step forward with left foot, turning slightly left (slow).
5. Step to right side with right foot (quick).
6. Bring left foot next to right (quick).

The Rumba Breaks

THE MOST colorful steps in Rumba are the patterns called Breaks. They add life and vivacity to the dance by introducing sharper, more staccato movements.

These steps are called Breaks because they are emphasized footsteps that break the smooth, even tempo and accent it. However, even though the Break movements are stressed, *they must still be done with Rumba motion* to be in keeping with the music.

The Forward Break, Man's Part

1. Step forward with left foot, bending left knee and keeping weight on right. Accent that step (slow).
2. Bring right foot, bending right knee, next to left, with weight on left (quick).
3. Step in place with left foot, left knee bent and weight on right (quick).

The girl's part, when the man leads a Forward Break, is the direct opposite. She starts back with her right foot, right knee bent, weight on left, and accents that first step.

The Backward Break, Man's Part

Since the Back Break is most often used following a Forward Break, use it in this manner as you learn it.

1. Shift weight to left foot as you step back with right foot, bending right knee. Accent that step (slow).
2. Bring left foot with left knee bent, next to right, weight on right (quick).
3. Step in place with right foot, right knee bent and weight on left (quick).

The girl's part, again, is the direct opposite.

Combination of Forward and Back Rumba Breaks

MAN'S PART

1, 2, 3. Same as Forward Rumba Break, facing page.

4, 5, 6. Back Rumba Break starting back with right foot.

GIRL: Step back with right foot on count 1; step forward with *left* foot on count 4.

The Side Breaks in Rumba

First review "The Five Correct Positions of the Feet," pages 117-118.

MAN'S PART

1. Step to left side with left foot, dropping right hand in slightly open position.* Left knee should be bent and weight on right foot (slow).

2. Bring right foot *in fifth position behind left,* right knee bent, weight on left (quick).

3. Step in place with left foot, bending left knee and keeping weight on right (quick).

4. Shift weight to left foot and step to right side with right foot, dropping left hand in slightly open position.* Right knee should be bent and weight on left foot (slow).

5. Bring left foot *in fifth position behind right,* left knee bent, weight on right, and open your dance position slightly to the left (quick).

6. Step in place with right foot, right knee bent and weight on left (quick).

GIRL: Step to right side with right foot on count 1. Place left foot *in fifth position behind right* on count 2. Step to left side with left foot on count 4 and place right foot *in fifth position behind left on* 5.

* This open-position action can be likened to opening the pages of a book.

The Open Rumba Break

THE OPEN Rumba Break is a most effective-looking pattern. Since you have already learned the portions included in the full pattern, you should find it easy to master.

There are three things on which to concentrate: using Rumba motion in every step you take, accenting every slow count, and visualizing how to release the girl and lead her in open position. If you should need help, stop in at your nearest Arthur Murray studio for a complimentary demonstration of this Rumba style.

Before starting, review the Left Box Turn and the Rumba Box Step. Remember that Cuban *Rhythm* is counted slow, quick, quick.

MAN'S PART

1, 2, 3. Release your right hand hold of your partner on count 1 and lead her with your left hand to take the first three counts of the Left Box Turn in open position as you step left, right, left.

4, 5, 6. Lead your partner to go forward as you step back right, left, right, *in Cuban Rhythm*, circling to your right. (See picture on facing page.)

1, 2, 3. Continue stepping back in Cuban Rhythm — left, right, left — still circling to your right.

4, 5, 6. Bring your partner back to closed position as you use counts 4, 5, 6 of the Rumba Box Step.

GIRL'S PART when a man leads the Open Rumba Break

STUDY THE MAN'S part on the facing page before you attempt your own part.

1, 2, 3. As man drops his right hand in the open position shown in the illustration, he will lead you to step into the first three counts of the girl's part of the Left Box Turn, starting back right.

4, 5, 6. The man will lead you to progress forward, circling right and still in Cuban Rhythm, stepping left, right, left.

1, 2, 3. You will continue being led in forward Cuban Rhythm, circling right and stepping right, left, right.

4, 5, 6. The man will resume regular closed dancing position as he leads you in counts 4, 5, 6 of the girl's part of the Rumba Box Step.

The Back Spot Turn in Rumba

A BACK SPOT TURN is popular with all advanced Rumba dancers. You will need to devote concentrated practice, but, since the pattern is fun to dance and most effective in appearance, it is worth spending time to learn it.

The turn itself is always used as a portion of a linked pattern. The following description will give you a particularly smooth sequence of movement.

MAN'S PART

Use Cuban Rhythm count of slow, quick, quick throughout entire pattern.

Two measures (six counts) Rumba Box Step.

Three measures (nine counts) starting with left foot, take nine steps backward as you circle, turning right. See picture on facing page.

One measure (three counts) Rumba Side Break to the right.

Two measures (six counts) Rumba Box Step.

Caution! As you take your nine steps backward, do so *walking* in Cuban Rhythm. Do not cross your feet.

Remember that to turn right you glance over your right shoulder. After you have achieved the Back Spot Turn to music, try turning more sharply, in a smaller circle.

**GIRL'S PART when a man leads
the Back Spot Turn in Rumba**

WITH THE Back Spot Turn combination described on the facing
page, it will be especially helpful for you to learn the man's part
first. As you practice it, imagine that you are leading someone.
This will give you a clearer picture of how you will be led.

Your part will be the direct opposite of the man's. In the nine
counts of the turn itself, you will walk forward in Cuban
Rhythm, starting with your right foot and circling right. Do not
be timid in taking forward steps. If you step reluctantly, in fear
of treading on your partner's toes, it will make your dancing
feel heavy and lifeless.

Part Five

THE MAMBO

The Mambo

THE MAMBO is a combination of Cuban Rumba with the syncopation found in Swing Fox Trot. So Mambo can truly be called a Latin-American dance.

Mambo music uses the same distinctive drum and gourd instruments as the Rumba; it is also in 4/4 time, but the syncopated beat adds a different count for dancers. We count Rumba as slow, quick, quick — the slow count taking twice as long as a quick and thus totaling four beats to each measure. Mambo is also counted in four beats to a measure, but the rhythm is quick, quick, *hold,* quick. No step is taken on the "hold" count. Thus, both Rumba and Mambo use four beats to a measure but take only three footsteps.

Before you start learning the Mambo, you will find it helpful to listen to several full recordings of the music. Try counting the measures aloud either as 1, 2, 3, 4 or quick, quick, hold, quick.

It is important that you remember to use Rumba motion in every Mambo step pattern that you learn. When you want to make sure that you are incorporating Rumba motion, test yourself by placing your hands on your hips.

Mambo, pronounced as though it were spelled Mom-bo, is performed by expert dancers according to their individual temperament. The more conventional type of dancer retains closed, partnership position in almost all steps. Others, who enjoy flamboyant antics, add improvisations during which the partners separate and dance apart, facing each other, as you will see on the opposite page.

The above picture shows the solo style I mentioned, and, since all the various Mambo patterns — in closed or open dancing position — stem from the same foundation count and the same basic footwork, I advise you to spend adequate time in perfecting these lessons. Once you have learned how to move to the Mambo tempo, you will not only find the dance to be captivating and fascinating, but you will enjoy creating your own interpretation of the dance in time to music.

Mambo comes more naturally to Americans than the Rumba — it exemplifies our zest for enjoyment and our ability to adapt foreign rhythms and make them truly our own.

The Basic Mambo Step

THERE ARE two portions to the Basic Mambo Step — forward and back. This page gives you directions for the forward portion.

As already mentioned, you can count a Mambo measure either as quick, quick, hold, quick or as 1, 2, 3 (*a hold, not a step*), 4. The accent is on count 4.

MAN'S PART

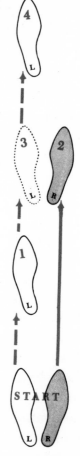

START

1. Step forward with left foot (quick).
2. Step forward with right foot (quick).
3. Pause with left foot, no weight on left (hold).
4. Step forward with left foot, accenting that step (quick).

Here is the back portion of the Basic Mambo Step. The two parts combine to form a very useful pattern done in place or turning gradually to the left.

MAN'S PART   Foot position at end of forward portion on facing page

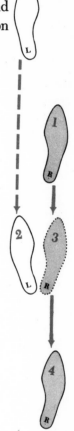

START

1. Step back with right foot. (This quick step is actually taken in place as it retraces footprint 2 of the forward portion.)
2. Step back with left foot (quick).
3. Pause with right foot, no weight on right (hold).
4. Step back with right foot, accenting that step (quick).

GIRL'S PART: When a man leads the full pattern of the Basic Mambo Step, the girl's part is the direct opposite. As he goes forward, she steps back, starting with her *right* foot. As he goes back, she steps forward, starting with her *left* foot.

Read the full description of the man's part to learn counts and accents.

The Box Step in the Mambo

YOU HAVE already learned the Box Step in the Waltz and in the Rumba. In both cases the footprint pattern was alike — the only difference was in the Rumba motion and the accent.

But in Mambo, the "Box Step" does not adhere to the squared-off pattern. The final count of each measure is accented by stepping forward or back.

The diagram on this page shows *the forward half* of the Mambo Box. Remember that count 3 is a "hold."

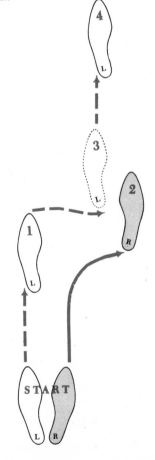

MAN'S PART

START

1. Step forward with left foot (quick).
2. Step diagonally forward with right foot (quick).
3. Follow through with left foot, no weight on left (hold).
4. Step forward with left foot, accenting that step (quick).

When you are sure that you have accomplished the forward half of the Mambo Box Step described on the facing page, follow it with the backward half to complete the pattern.

Remember that at the start of the back half of the Mambo Box Step the man's left foot is forward, weight on that foot.

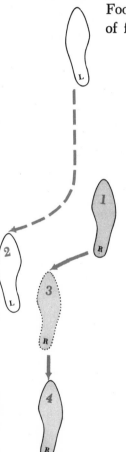

Foot position at end of forward half

MAN'S PART

START

1. Step back with right foot. (This quick step is actually taken in place as it retraces footprint 2 of the forward half of the Mambo Box.)
2. Step diagonally back to the left side with the left foot (quick).
3. Follow through with right foot, no weight on right (hold).
4. Step back with right foot, accenting that step (quick).

After achieving the full Mambo Box, practice it turning left on each count of one.

GIRL: The girl's part is the direct opposite. As the man dances the forward half of the Box, the girl starts back on her right foot. As he dances the back half of the Box, she starts forward on her *left* foot.

Forward and Back Mambo Breaks

As I mentioned previously, a Break is an emphasized, accented footstep. In this Forward and Back Mambo Break, the accent is placed on each count of four.

Here is the Forward half of this combination Break. Count it as 1, 2, 3, 4 or quick, quick, hold, quick.

MAN'S PART

START

1. Step forward with left foot (quick).
2, 3. Bring right foot next to left, weight on right, and hold (quick, hold).
4. Step forward with left foot, accenting the step (quick).

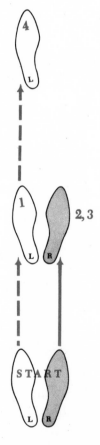

This is the Back half that follows the portion given on the facing page.

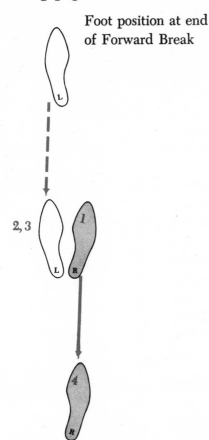

Foot position at end of Forward Break

MAN'S PART

START

1. Step back with right foot. (This quick step is actually taken in place as it retraces footprint 2 of the forward portion.)
2, 3. Bring left foot next to right, weight on left, and hold (quick and hold).
4. Step back with right foot, accenting that step (quick).

GIRL: The girl's part is the direct opposite of the man's. As he dances the Forward half, she starts back with her right foot. For the Back half, she starts *forward* with her *left* foot.

Mambo Turn

Repeat the combined Forward and Back Mambo Breaks, turning left on each count of one. Turn left only.

The Open Break in Mambo

THE OPEN BREAK, a very popular Mambo step, includes the open dance position that you have already learned in the Open Rumba Break. Review page 132.

MAN'S PART

START

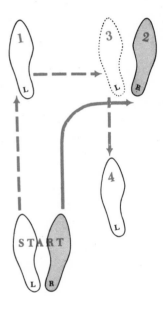

1. Step forward with left foot, releasing right hand hold of partner in open position (quick).
2. Step to the right side with right foot (quick).
3. Brush left foot next to right, no weight on left (hold).
4. Step back with left foot, accenting that step (quick).

IMPORTANT: The above Open Break must be followed by another portion to complete a full pattern, for two reasons:

  a. It ends with a left footstep for the man.

  b. It ends with partners in open position.

Therefore, follow the Open Break by closing into regular dance position with the second half of the Mambo Box Step. For the man, this starts in place with right foot.

LEADING: Read the girl's part, facing page. Note that as the man steps *back* with his left foot on count 4 of the Open Break portion, the girl must be led to also step *back* with her right foot.

GIRL'S PART when a man leads the Open Break in Mambo

Read the entire facing page and study that diagram.

GIRL'S PART

START

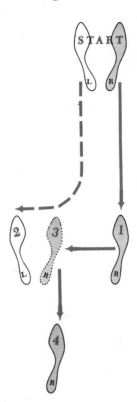

1. Step back with right foot as your partner releases you in open position (quick).
2. Step to the left side with your left foot (quick).
3. Brush right foot next to left, no weight on right (hold).
4. Step *back* with right foot, accenting that step (quick).

Follow the above Open Break with girl's part of the second half of the Mambo Box Step, which starts forward with left foot.

While practicing Mambo, exaggerate the emphasis on every fourth, accented count. And, while learning any pattern in open dance position, try to visualize how you will be led.

Open Mambo Break with Underarm Turn

THIS IS a very effective-looking Mambo pattern that you will thoroughly enjoy using.

I have divided the description into three portions. You already know the first portion, which is the Open Mambo Break. The second portion is the Underarm Turn, illustrated on the facing page. The final portion is the entire Mambo Box Step, which you have also already learned.

MAN'S PART

First Portion, four counts. Open Mambo Break.
Second Portion, four counts.

Maintain the open dance position of the Break and lead .girl to walk forward under your left arm as shown in the drawing as you step:

1. In place with right foot (quick).
2. Bring left foot next to right (quick).
3. Pause in place (hold).
4. Step back with right foot, accenting that step (quick).

Third Portion, eight counts: Resume regular dance position as you lead entire Mambo Box Step.

GIRL'S PART when a man leads
the Open Mambo Break with Underarm Turn

First Portion, four counts. Girl's part of Open Mambo Break.
Second Portion, four counts. As man releases his right arm from your waist and leads you to turn under his arm, *you step forward, turning sharply to your right in a small circle,* with:

1. Forward left (quick).
2. Forward right (quick).
3. Pause in place (hold).
4. Forward left (quick).

Third Portion, eight counts. Girl's part of entire Mambo Box Step.

Forward Spot Turn in Mambo

A SPOT TURN consists of walking steps taken either forward or back, in a sharply turned circle.

While learning the Forward Spot Turn in Mambo, master the pattern first. Then, after you can dance it with the music, practice until you can achieve a sharper turn.

MAN'S PART

Take all steps circling left. See illustration.
1. Step forward with left foot (quick).
2. Step forward with right foot (quick).
3. Pause in place (hold).
4. Step forward with left foot (quick).

Repeat, thus totaling two measures and ending with a forward step on right foot.

How to Use the Forward Spot Turn in Mambo

Here is an effective series of step patterns for a man to lead.

First Portion: Entire Mambo Box. (For advanced styling turn sharply to your left on counts 2 and 4.)

Second Portion: Two measures of Forward Spot Turn as described above.

Third Portion: Two measures using Basic Mambo Breaks, Forward and Back.

GIRL'S PART when a man leads
a Forward Spot Turn in Mambo

IT IS ESSENTIAL that you study the man's part of the Forward Spot Turn, on the facing page. After you can dance the man's part to music, try your own part, which is the direct opposite. You will start back with your right foot, *circling left*.

After you have mastered your part of the Spot Turn, practice the girl's part of the *series* of step patterns, starting with the Mambo Box.

Part Six

THE CHA-CHA

The Cha-Cha

THE CHA-CHA is the newest and the most popular of the Latin-American dances. It is also the easiest to learn because the music has a definite and unmistakable beat.

However, although you should be able to master the basic patterns very quickly, you will need time to achieve attractive style in the dance. A good Cha-Cha dancer uses Rumba motion in almost all of the steps.

Before studying the Basic Cha-Cha pattern on the facing page, first learn how to count in this dance.

How to Count the Cha-Cha

THERE ARE two ways to count Cha-Cha rhythm. Both are correct; so, as you are learning a pattern, use whichever count you prefer.

You may count 1, 2, 3, 4-and.

OR:

You may count 1, 2, 3, Cha-Cha.

Practice counting aloud to a slow- or medium-tempo Cha-Cha.

Accent count 2 of each measure.

The Basic Cha-Cha

First Half

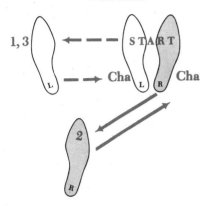

Second Half

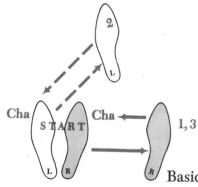

MAN'S PART

START

1. Step to left side with left foot.
2. Step back with right foot, accenting that step.
3. Step in place with left foot.

4-and (or Cha-Cha). Step to right side with right foot and bring left foot next to right, weight on left.

1. Step to right side with right foot.
2. Step forward with left foot, accenting that step.
3. Step in place with right foot.

4-and (or Cha-Cha). Step to left side with left foot and bring right foot next to left, weight on right.

Basic Cha-Cha is an especially useful pattern. Since the count and accent are entirely different from the other dances you have studied, devote sufficient time to mastering it. Use slow or medium tempo of music before trying a faster speed.

After you have achieved Basic Cha-Cha, use the entire pattern, turning to your left.

NOTE: Many Cha-Cha patterns start with the *first half* of the Basic Step. Be sure you know the separate halves.

GIRL'S PART when a man leads
the Basic Cha-Cha

PLEASE READ the entire preceding page describing the man's part of the Basic Cha-Cha. Practice counting aloud to slow- or medium-tempo music before trying your own part of the pattern.

First Half

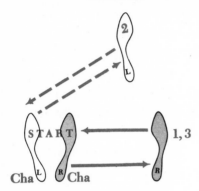

GIRL'S PART

START

1. Step to right side with right foot.
2. Step *forward* with left foot, accenting.
3. Step in place with left foot.
4-and (or Cha-Cha). Step to left side with left foot and bring right foot next to left, weight on right.

Second Half

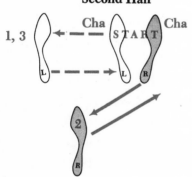

1. Step to left side with left foot.
2. Step back with right foot, accenting.
3. Step in place with left foot.
4-and (or Cha-Cha). Step to right side with right foot and bring left foot next to right, weight on left.

The Open Break in Cha-Cha

THIS IS A universally popular Cha-Cha variation. It uses the open dance position that you have already learned in both the Rumba and Mambo Open Breaks.

In this pattern, *both man and girl should read and study each other's part*. I advise this since the girl's footwork in the second half of the step is not the direct opposite of the man's.

MAN'S PART

First Half: First half of Basic Cha-Cha, releasing right hand
   hold of partner on the 4-and (or Cha-Cha) count.
Second Half:
   1. Step to right side with right foot.
   2. Step *back* with left foot, accenting that step.
   3. Step in place with right foot.
   4-and (or Cha-Cha). Step to left side with left foot and
      bring right foot next to left, weight on right.
         Accent each count of two!

GIRL'S PART

First Half: First half of girl's part of Basic Cha-Cha.
Second Half: Second half of girl's part of Basic Cha-Cha. Note
   that this means you will be stepping *back*, in open position,
   on count 2 while the man is also stepping *back*.

Conversation Back Break In Cha-Cha

You WILL enjoy dancing the Conversation Back Break in Cha-Cha because it is easy to learn and easy to lead, yet looks advanced and intricate.

Should you be in doubt about the style or pattern of this or any other Cha-Cha step, stop in at your nearest Arthur Murray Studio for a complimentary demonstration.

MAN'S PART

First Half: First half of Basic Cha-Cha.
Second Half:

1. Step to right side with right foot, releasing girl into Conversation position.
2. Step back with left foot, maintaining Conversation position. (See illustration on facing page.)
3. Step in place with right foot.

4-and (or Cha-Cha). Return to regular dance position as you step to left side with left foot and bring right foot next to left, weight on right.

GIRL'S PART when a man leads
the Conversation Back Break in Cha-Cha

First Half: First half of girl's part of Basic Cha-Cha.
Second Half:

1. Step to left side with left foot as man releases you into Conversation position.
2. Step back with right foot while in Conversation position. (See illustration.)
3. Step in place with left foot.
4-and (or Cha-Cha). As you are led back to regular dance position, step to right side with right foot and bring left foot next to right, weight on left.

The Cross-over Break in Cha-Cha

THE CROSS-OVER BREAK is a pattern that every Cha-Cha dancer uses. It lends itself to many variations and improvisations.

MAN'S PART

First Measure. First half of Basic Cha-Cha, *releasing your right hand hold of your partner* on the 4-and (or Cha-Cha) count.

Second Measure.

1. Step forward with right foot, turning one quarter to your right.
2. Maintaining open position, step forward with left foot, *accenting that "Break"* step. (See top illustration, facing page.)
3. Step back with right foot to again face partner.

4-and (or Cha-Cha). Step to left side with left foot; bring right foot next to left *and change hands.* (Take the girl's left hand in your right hand.)

Third Measure.

1. Step forward with left foot, turning one quarter to your left.
2. Maintaining open position, step forward with right foot, *accenting that "Break"* step. (See lower illustration, facing page.)
3. Step back with left foot to again face partner.

4-and (or Cha-Cha). Step to right side with right foot; bring left foot next to right *and change hands.* (Take the girl's right hand in your left hand.)

Fourth Measure. Repeat Second Measure, *but do not change hands on the 4-and (Cha-Cha) count.*

Fifth and Sixth Measures. Entire Basic Cha-Cha Step.

GIRL: Your part of the Cross-over Break is the direct opposite of the man's. You will be able to follow this step easily if you first learn the man's part thoroughly enough to lead it.

Part Seven

THE TANGO

The Tango

FOR MANY YEARS, the Tango has been danced by professionals in a very elaborate manner. They have made it appear to be a highly advanced, complicated dance. As a result of seeing such exhibitions, many people have felt that the Tango was far beyond their ability, and have therefore been reluctant to try it.

The original Tango, which came from the Argentine, *was* a difficult dance, and the French adaptation of it was almost as involved. The Americanized version, however, is a very simple ballroom dance which you should have no trouble at all in learning.

The steps are somewhat similar to those used in the Waltz and the Fox Trot, and I have arranged the instructions so that anyone who has mastered these dances will be able to go on easily to the Tango.

Why You Should Learn to Tango

ANYONE who wants to become a really good dancer should learn to Tango. Even if Tango is not commonly danced in your community, you will benefit by practicing the patterns to music.

In no other dance is there a more definite, marked musical beat. Keeping time to Tango will not only develop a finer sense of rhythm but will also train your feet to respond, almost automatically, to melody. In addition, the slow and quick counts used in Tango patterns will teach the muscular control you need for graceful change of weight. The glamorous Tango is indeed a useful and valuable dance!

Tango Rhythm

I HAVE FOUND that all students learn Tango tempo more readily when they count aloud in "slows" and "quicks" rather than in numbers. Try this whenever you begin to study a new pattern.

If you play Tango music and listen to it, you will hear the beats quite readily. When you dance, a "quick" count takes one beat, a "slow" count takes two.

There is also a pause in most Tango patterns. For this we count "hold," and it is equivalent in time to a "quick." It is the slow-quick and the quick-hold variations that give the Tango its individuality as a ballroom dance.

The Forward Promenade in Tango

THE FORWARD PROMENADE is a basic Tango step pattern, useful to both beginners and advanced dancers. The foot movements are easy to learn, but you must concentrate on the correct count of slow, slow, quick, quick, quick-hold. Count aloud, taking twice as long for a "slow" as for a "quick." The "hold" is equal to a "quick."

Remember! Do not place your weight when a dotted footprint is shown in the diagram.

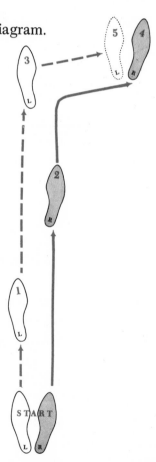

MAN'S PART

START

1. Forward with left foot (slow).
2. Forward with right foot (slow).
3. Forward with left foot (quick).
4. Step to right side with right foot (quick).
5. Bring left foot next to right, *no weight on left,* and pause (quick-hold).

After you can dance the Forward Promenade in time to music, practice it in continuous repetition around the room in the Line of Direction. Be sure you do not place your weight on the "quick-hold" counts.

GIRL'S PART when a man leads
the Forward Promenade in Tango

READ THE ENTIRE facing page carefully so that you will fully understand the correct count. Then, since it is easier to learn a pattern that starts forward, study the man's part before your own.

GIRL'S PART

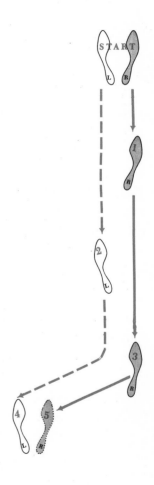

START

1. Step back with right foot (slow).
2. Step back with left foot (slow).
3. Step back with right foot (quick).
4. Step to left side with left foot (quick).
5. Bring right foot next to left, *no weight on right* and pause (quick-hold).

When you are sure of the step pattern and can dance it in time to music, practice by repeating it continuously, moving backward around the room in the Line of Direction.

Forward Promenade in Tango Variation in Right Parallel Position

THE FORWARD PROMENADE, described on the previous page, takes on an entirely different appearance when the man leads his partner into Right Parallel position on the second step.

MAN'S PART

Imagine yourself leading a partner. You would start in regular dance position as you step forward with your left foot (slow).

As you take your second step, which is forward with your right foot (slow), you would place your partner as shown in the drawing on the facing page. That is Right Parallel position.

On your next step, which is forward with your left foot (quick), you would bring her back to regular dance position and would finish the pattern in that manner.

GIRL: The girl merely follows, using her part of the Promenade. It is up to the man to lead her from regular dance position into Right Parallel and then bring her back. A girl can get a clearer picture of this advanced variation by trying the man's part.

The El Sharon Promenade in Tango

THIS IS one of the most popular Tango steps. It should be used several times in succession; the change in dance position prevents any feeling of monotony.

Note that on count 2 the man leads his partner in Conversation position. He returns her to regular closed position on count 3 to finish the pattern. (Review the Conversation Step in Fox Trot, pages 66 through 69.)

Place no weight when the diagram shows a dotted footprint!

MAN'S PART

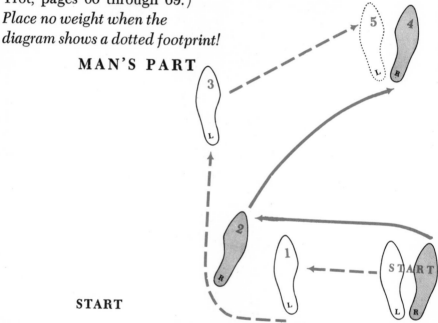

START

1. Step to left side with left foot (slow).
2. Cross right foot in front of left in Conversation position (slow).
3. Step forward with left foot leading girl back to regular dance position (quick).
4. Step to right side with right foot (quick).
5. Bring left foot next to right, *no weight on left,* and pause (quick-hold).

GIRL'S PART when a man leads
the El Sharon Promenade in Tango

PLEASE READ the description of the man's part on the facing page. Note that the count is the same as you have already learned — slow, slow, quick, quick, quick-hold.

Remember that you do not place your weight on a step shown by a dotted footprint.

GIRL'S PART

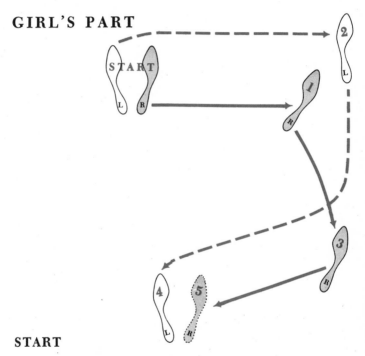

START

1. Step to right side with right foot (slow).
2. Cross left foot in front of right (slow). On this step, the man will be leading you into Conversation position.
3. Step back with right foot (quick).
4. Step to left side with left foot (quick).
5. Bring right foot next to left, *no weight on right,* and pause (quick-hold).

The Corté in the Tango

THE CORTÉ (pronounced as though spelled Cor-tay) is a dip step that is taken backward by the man. His entire weight is placed on the back-stepping foot; that knee is bent and the forward foot is raised slightly from the floor.

Count slow, slow, quick, quick, quick-hold.

MAN'S PART

START

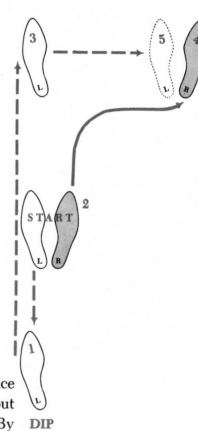

1. Step back with left foot in a dip, bending left knee and placing entire weight on left foot (slow).
2. Step forward with right foot (slow). This step is actually taken in place, since you merely lower the foot you have slightly raised.
3. Step forward with left foot (quick).
4. Step to right side with right foot (quick).
5. Bring left foot next to right, *no weight on left,* and pause (quick-hold).

After mastering the pattern, practice it with the variation of turning about one quarter to the left on count 3. By successively repeating the pattern you can thus make a complete turn to again face the Line of Direction.

GIRL'S PART when a man leads
the Corté in the Tango

THE CORTÉ is an attractive-looking step when a girl has learned
how to dip gracefully. To achieve this, *learn the man's pattern
first*. Practice it as though you were leading a partner. This will
help you to visualize how to follow a dip step.

In actual dancing, remember rule one for good balance — to
take a firm hold with your left hand just in back of your partner's
right shoulder. You will then find it easy to dip forward lightly.

GIRL'S PART

START

1. Step forward with right foot
   in a dip, bending right
   knee and placing entire
   weight on right foot
   (slow).
2. Step back with left foot
   (slow). This step is actually taken in place,
   since you merely lower
   the foot you have slightly raised.
3. Step back with right foot
   (quick).
4. Step to left side with left
   foot (quick).
5. Bring right foot next to left,
   no weight on right, and
   pause (quick-hold).

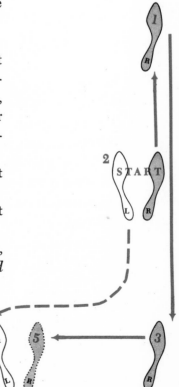

The Argentine Walk in Tango

HERE IS an attractive Tango walking step that is taken in the Line of Direction, progressing forward around the room.

It introduces a Tango count which you have not yet learned.

MAN'S PART

First Portion: Count slow, slow, quick, quick.
1. Forward with left foot (slow).
2. Forward with right foot (slow). See illustration.
3. Forward with left foot (quick).
4. Follow through and step to right side with right foot, weight on right (quick).

Second Portion: Repeat first portion.

Third Portion:
1. Forward with left foot (quick).
2. Follow through and step to right side with right foot (quick).
3. Bring left foot next to right, no weight on left, and pause (quick-hold).

GIRL: The girl's part is the exact reverse of the man's.

Contrabody Motion in Tango

IN TANGO, more than in any other ballroom dance, good dancers enhance their appearance with the style that is often called Contrabody Motion.

Study the description on this page. Then review the Tango patterns you have learned and add this advanced styling pointer during your practice.

As you step forward with your left foot, bring your right shoulder slightly forward as shown in the drawing.

As you step forward with your right foot, bring your left shoulder slightly forward as shown.

Part Eight

THE SAMBA

The Samba

OF THE POPULAR Latin-American dances, the Samba is undoubtedly the gayest and most lighthearted of all. It originated in Brazil, where it gradually developed from an almost barbaric carnival dance into its present graceful ballroom style. The music, however, still retains the high-spirited abandon of the *fiesta.*

The distinctive characteristic of Samba is a smooth up-and-down knee motion taken, with few exceptions, on every count of the music. The step patterns are easy to learn; it is the Samba motion of each step that will require practice.

Samba Motion

> Stand with feet together.
> Practice in place, rising on toes with knees straight and then bending both knees at the same time. Count and-1, and-2. Rise on the toes on every count of "and" and bend both knees on the numbered counts 1, 2.

Exaggerate your knee action at the start; with practice you can gradually attain a smooth, effortless appearance.

Be sure to continue practicing in place until you can keep time to the music.

Footstep Pattern of Basic Samba

For PRELIMINARY study, it is essential that you first know the footprint pattern of Basic Samba before you can learn to dance it in Samba tempo. So, temporarily, omit any attempt to use Samba motion.

Do not be discouraged by this page of elementary instruction; you will find it far easier to master Samba style for the pattern once you know the positions of the feet.

This is the man's part. *Learn it, for the present, without any counts or music.* Girls, too, should learn this portion.

Forward:
    Start with feet together.
    Step forward with left foot.
    Bring right foot next to left, weight on right.
    Step in place with left foot.

Back:
    Step back with right foot.
    Bring left foot next to right, weight on left.
    Step in place with right foot.

Despite the simplicity of this pattern, repeat it until you have achieved smooth change of weight. Do not attempt the next page until you can move forward and back almost automatically.

Basic Samba Using Samba Motion

THIS IS how to dance the man's part of the step pattern described on the previous page, in Samba tempo and style.

Reread the description of Samba motion, page 178. In Basic Samba, you should rise on toes with knees straight on every count of "and." Bend both knees on every numbered count (1, 2, etc.).

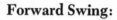

Forward Swing:
Bounce forward with left foot (and-1).
Bring right foot next to left with weight on right and step in place with left foot (and-2).
Knees should flex twice during this forward portion.

Backward Swing:
Bounce back with right foot (and-3).
Bring left foot next to right with weight on left and step in place with right foot (and-4).
Flex knees twice during this backward portion.

The Waltz Steps in Samba

REVIEW the Forward and Back Waltz Steps, pages 86 through 89. These steps are easily adapted to Samba. The *patterns* are the same, but they look entirely different due to the count, the motion and the shorter side steps.

Forward Waltz in Samba

KNEES straighten and bend on every double count, such as and-1.

MAN'S PART

Bounce forward on left foot (and-1).

Very short step to right side and bring left next to right, weight on left (and-2).

Bounce forward on right foot (and-3).

Very short step to left side and bring right next to left, weight on right (and-4).

Repeat.

Backward Waltz in Samba

Continue knee straightening and bending on every double count.

MAN'S PART

Bounce back on left foot (and-1).

Very short step to right side and bring left next to right, weight on left (and-2).

Bounce back on right foot (and-3).

Very short step to left side and bring right next to left, weight on right (and-4).

Repeat.

Practice Pattern: Entire Forward Waltz Step in Samba danced twice in succession followed by entire Backward Waltz also danced twice (sixteen double counts).

The Two-way Chassé in Samba

ONCE YOU have achieved Samba motion and practiced it in the forward and back Basic Samba, you will find it easy to master this pattern. It includes the Chassé, which is the side-close step you have already learned. (See page 52.)

Straighten and bend both knees on every double count of and-1, and-2, etc.

MAN'S PART

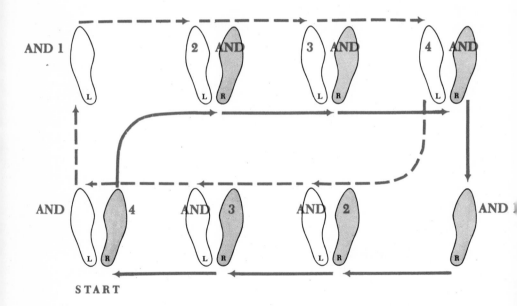

Start with feet together.
Bounce forward with left foot (and-1).
Chassé to right side (and-2).
Chassé to right side twice more (and-3, and-4).
Bounce back with right foot (and-1).
Chassé to left side (and-2).
Chassé to left side twice more (and-3, and-4).

GIRL'S PART when a man leads
the Two-Way Chassé in Samba

Read entire facing page.

When learning a new Samba pattern, always begin by flexing your knees in place first. This will help to start you off in correct, bouncing action. In the Two-Way Chassé, continue to straighten and bend your knees during every double count of and-1, and-2, etc.

GIRL'S PART

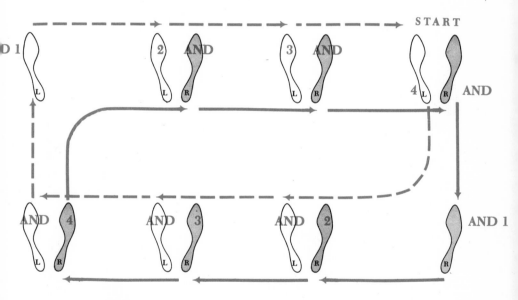

Start with feet together.
Bounce back with right foot (and-1).
Chassé to left side (and-2).
Chassé to left side twice more (and-3, and-4).
Bounce forward with left foot (and-1).
Chassé to right side (and-2).
Chassé to right side twice more (and-3, and-4).

The Balancetes

THIS BALANCE pattern is a very attractive Samba step and is particularly useful on a crowded floor. Again, in this pattern you should straighten and bend knees on every double count of and-1, and-2, etc.

Balancete to the Left

MAN'S PART

Bounce to left side with left foot (and-1). Step right foot in fifth position in back of left, immediately returning weight to To the left   left foot (and-2). See illustration.

Balancete to the Right

MAN'S PART

Bounce to right side with right foot (and-3).
Step left foot in fifth position in back of right, immediately returning weight to right foot (and-4). See illustration.   To the right

GIRL: The girl also crosses *in back* in fifth position as shown in the illustrations.

The Paulista in Samba

First learn the footprint pattern of the Paulista, without counts or music.

MAN'S PART

Step forward with left foot, turning slightly left.

Step to right side with right foot, *placing entire weight on toes.*

Step in place with left foot, weight on left.

Repeat same movement, starting forward with right foot.

How to Dance the Paulista in Samba Style

RISE, straightening knees on every "and"; bend knees on every 1, 2, etc.

Bounce forward with left foot, turning slightly left (and-1).

Step to right side with right foot, weight on right toes, and immediately step in place with left foot, weight on left (and-2). Rise on the side step, *bend knees as you step in place.*

Repeat, starting forward with right foot and turning slightly right.

LEAD: On counts and-2, girl must be led to step *back*, swinging away from her partner, and then to step in place. Thus the couple perform in a circular sweep from left to right. See illustration.

The Copacabana in Samba

THE COPACABANA is a series of rocking steps progressing forward in Conversation position. See illustration, facing page. Because the pattern is exceptionally attractive and fun to do, it will be well worth your learning it thoroughly.

First become completely familiar with the footwork. *Learn it without counts and without music.*

Footprint Pattern of the Copa

MAN'S PART

Turn girl to Conversation position and step:

Forward with left foot.

Backward with right foot, weight on right.

Forward with left foot, weight on left. (Note that this footstep is actually taken "in place," as the left foot is still advanced.)

Forward with right foot.

Backward with left foot, weight on left.

Forward with right foot, weight on right. (Again, this step is actually taken "in place.")

How to Dance the Copa in Samba Style

BOTH KNEES should be straightened on every count of "and"; both should bend on every numbered count (1, 2, etc.).

MAN'S PART

Precede the Copa steps with a Balancete to the left and a Balancete to the right, opening to Conversation position.
Now use the footstep pattern described on facing page.
Bounce forward with left foot, *tipping body slightly back* (and-1).
Step back with right foot, weight on right, *knees straight and tipping body forward;* then immediately step forward with left foot, weight on left, knees bent (and-2).
Repeat, starting forward with right foot (and-3, and-4).

> You may stop in at your nearest Arthur Murray Studio for a complimentary demonstration of Copa and other Samba patterns.

GIRL: Your part is exactly the same as the man's except that you will be starting forward with your right foot when he is stepping forward with his left.

The Reverse Copacabana

MAN'S PART

First Portion: Balancete to left side, releasing girl to the open position shown above. (Review Balancete, page 184.)

Second Portion: In open position, take five Copacabana steps forward, starting with right foot. (Each Copa step will take count of and-1, and-2.)

Tip body back and forward as described on the previous page.

Third Portion: Forward Waltz step in Samba style turning one quarter left and closing to regular dance position.

To add style: During the five Copacabana steps, turn body slightly right when stepping forward on right foot. Turn body slightly left when stepping forward on left foot.

Part Nine

THE MERENGUE

The Merengue

THE MERENGUE is the most recent Latin-American dance to become popular. It originated in the West Indies, where it gradually changed through the years from a wild, half-savage folk dance to its present sophisticated ballroom version.

In some sections, such as Haiti, Merengue is pronounced Mareng; in others, as Ma-reng-gay, with the accent on the last syllable. Either is correct. But no matter how the name is pronounced, the basic quality of the dance is exactly the same.

The "Lame-Duck" Styling of Merengue

THE CHIEF characteristic that makes Merengue different from any other ballroom dance is a "lame-duck" motion — that is, a step taken with a slight limp.

If you have never seen the Merengue danced, you will be cordially welcome to a complimentary showing at your nearest Arthur Murray Studio.

In Merengue, you step to every beat of the music, and the lame-duck styling is used on the odd-number counts of most patterns (counts 1, 3, 5, 7). All steps are taken with a bright, staccato tempo *and with Rumba hip motion.* This is essential.

Basic Merengue to the Side

SIDE STEPS or Chassés are used in many Merengue patterns.

As you learn Basic Merengue to the side, emphasize the lame-duck styling on all odd counts (1, 3, 5, 7), as shown in the illustration.

Note placement of hips when the step is taken correctly, with Rumba motion. Practice in this manner.

MAN'S PART

1. Step to left side with left foot, weight on right.
   Bend left knee slightly and dip left shoulder.
2. Shift weight to left foot and bring right foot next to left.
   Repeat to a total of eight counts.

GIRL: Your part is the direct opposite. Start to the right side with your right foot, weight on left.

Basic Merengue Forward

IN THE Basic Merengue progressing forward, continue to use the lame-duck style on the odd counts and on those accented counts 1, 3, 5 and 7 take a long step. Take a very short step on the even counts. Use Rumba motion on every step.

MAN'S PART

START

1. Long step forward with left foot, left knee bent and weight on right.
2. Shift weight to left foot and take short step forward with right foot, right knee bent.

Repeat to a total of eight counts.

Practice Pattern

Eight counts of Basic Merengue Forward

Eight counts of Basic Merengue to the side

GIRL: When the man leads Basic Merengue Forward, you will start back on your right foot. Take long, accented steps on the odd counts.

The Stair Step in Merengue

THIS PATTERN is an attractive combination of the Side and Forward Basic Merengues.

Use Rumba motion on every step, but in this particular pattern *accent only counts 1 and 5 with the lame-duck styling.*

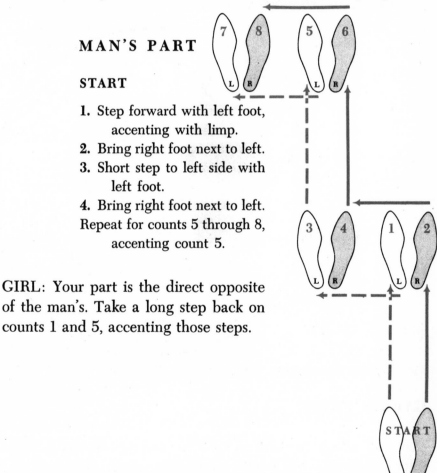

MAN'S PART

START

1. Step forward with left foot, accenting with limp.
2. Bring right foot next to left.
3. Short step to left side with left foot.
4. Bring right foot next to left.
Repeat for counts 5 through 8, accenting count 5.

GIRL: Your part is the direct opposite of the man's. Take a long step back on counts 1 and 5, accenting those steps.

Forward Spot Turn in Merengue

THE FORWARD Spot Turn in Merengue consists of eight forward walking steps, turning slightly left on each step to progress in a circle.

Take long steps on the accented counts 1, 3, 5, 7, using the lame-duck styling. Take short steps on the even counts. *Use Rumba motion throughout.*

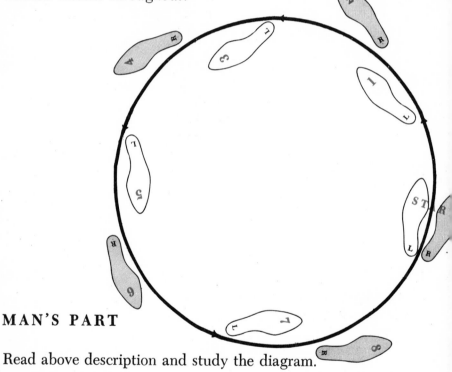

MAN'S PART

Read above description and study the diagram.

GIRL'S PART

Start with a long step back on right foot and turn slightly to your left on every step. Use Rumba motion throughout and accent the long steps on counts, 1, 3, 5 and 7.

Merengue Spot Turn
with Open Break

MAN'S PART

1–5. Use counts 1 through 5 of Forward Spot Turn on facing page.

6. Bring right foot next to left and release girl to open position.

7. Step back with left foot as you lead girl also to step back on her right foot. See illustration. Accent this "break" step.

8. Step forward with right foot, taking girl into regular, closed dancing position. (Follow through with left foot before starting next pattern.)

GIRL: Learn man's-part, which will make your own footwork easy to visualize.

The Pendulum Step in Merengue

FIRST LEARN the easy footprint pattern of the Pendulum. Then study the way to use it in Merengue style.

MAN'S PART

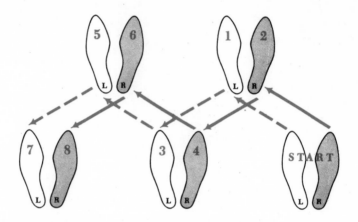

START

1. Step diagonally forward with left foot.
2. Bring right foot next to left, weight on right.
3. Step diagonally back with left foot.
4. Bring right foot next to left, weight on right.
Repeat for counts 5 through 8.

MERENGUE STYLE: Accent only the forward counts 1 and 5 with lame-duck motion. On the forward steps, tilt body back. On the backward steps, tilt body forward. Maintain Rumba motion throughout entire pattern.

GIRL: The girl's footprint pattern is the direct opposite. She starts diagonally back with right foot. As she steps back, her body should be tilted forward.

Part Ten

SWING

Swing

"SWING" is the general, all-inclusive term that is applied to syncopated Fox Trot dancing. Formerly called Jitterbug, Lindy Hop and various other names in different sections of the country, Swing is the newer title.

Syncopated or Swing music sets a different tempo from that with an evenly marked, regular beat, and it is irresistible to a good dancer. So although this type of dancing originated with very young people, the infectious gaiety of the music appeals to all ages.

Swing step patterns lend themselves to varied interpretation. Exuberant teen-agers like to use more exaggerated motions, while mature dancers prefer a quieter, more subtle style. However, the foundation Swing steps given in this chapter are standard basic patterns suitable for use in any ballroom, by youngsters or adults.

I advise everyone who wants to be a good dancer to learn Swing. The syncopated beat will give life to your footwork and the patterns will improve your balance and co-ordination through the quick changes of weight. For a man it offers excellent training in leading, and a girl who can follow Swing will be easier to lead in all other dances. Perhaps Christopher Morley had Swing in mind when he wrote: "Dancing is wonderful training for girls, it's the first way you learn to guess what a man is going to do before he does it."

Basic Swing Step

THE BASIC Swing Step uses the Magic Step count of slow, slow, quick, quick.

The first two "slow" counts are taken in regular dancing position. On the first "quick" count, the man leads his partner into the semiopen position shown in the illustration.

Note that arms are held low and that the man takes the *back* of the girl's right hand in his left hand. This is to facilitate spinning her or leading her into open, advanced steps.

MAN'S PART

1. Step to left side with left foot and brush right foot against left, no weight on right (slow).
2. Step to right side with right foot and brush left foot against right, no weight on left (slow).
3. Step back on left foot (quick). See illustration.
4. Step forward on right foot (quick).

After mastering Basic Swing in place, dance it turning right, gradually, on every step.

GIRL: The girl uses the same pattern as the man except that she starts to the right side. She, also, will step back-forward on "quick-quick."

How to Lead a Throw-out Break in Swing

MAN'S PART

First use one or more Basic Swing Steps, either in place or turning right. Description on preceding page.

Throw-out: Continue the footwork of Basic Swing, but on the first "slow" count release your right hand hold of your partner and lead her to the open position shown in the illustration.

NOTE: The girl's footwork in the Throw-out is entirely different from the man's. Study the facing page. By understanding the girl's part, you will find it easier to lead her.

How to Follow When a Man Leads a Throw-out Break in Swing

READ the man's part of a Throw-out Swing Break, on the facing page. Try his part for a clearer realization of what you must do to follow him.

When a Throw-out Break is done correctly, the girl must cover ground quickly in order to reach the open position shown in the picture. To do this, the girl uses what is called Triple Swing for her footwork.

What A Triple Means

A Triple has three very quick footsteps taken side, together, side. For instance, a Triple to the right would be to step to right side with right foot; step left foot next to right and again step to right side with right foot. A Triple to the left would be the same motions, but starting with the left foot.

In a Throw-out Break, the girl takes a Triple on each of the man's "slow" counts.

Also — *and this is important* — from an open position, the girl always steps forward, forward on the last two "quick" counts.

COUNT FOR GIRL: 1, 2, 3 . . . 1, 2, 3 . . . 1, 2. (Equal to slow, slow, quick, quick).

1, 2, 3. As man leads girl to open Throw-out position, she takes a Triple to the right side *while turning left*.

1, 2, 3. In open position, girl takes a Triple to the left side, staying in place.

1, 2. Step forward with right foot and forward with left, toward partner.

The Underarm Turn in Swing

THIS IS undoubtedly one of the most popular Swing steps. It looks difficult and advanced, but since you already know the first two portions, you should find the pattern easy to learn.

MAN'S PART

First Portion: Basic Swing in closed position.

Second Portion: Throw-out Break.

Third Portion: Man again does Basic Swing footwork in place, raising his left arm on the first "slow" count to turn girl under his arm to her left. See illustration.

Fourth Portion: Close to regular dance position with Basic Swing.

NOTE: Read the girl's part of this pattern. Her footwork differs from the man's in both the Throw-out Break and the Underarm Turn. It is easier to lead a girl when you know what she is meant to do.

Girl's Part of the Underarm Turn

Read all portions of the man's part of the Underarm Turn pattern.

You have already learned your part of all portions but the third. Study this carefully.

Third Portion, *for girl:*

Count 1, 2, 3 . . . 1, 2, 3 . . . 1, 2, as in Throw-out.

1, 2, 3 . . . 1, 2, 3. As man turns you under his arm, *to your left,* take a Triple to the right side and complete the turn with a Triple to the left side.

1, 2. Step forward with right foot and forward with left foot, toward your partner.

The Sugar Foot Walk in Swing

THE SUGAR FOOT WALK is a popular and typically Swing style movement for a girl. She must, however, be led into the Walk by her partner. It is used when partners separate, as in a Throw-out Break or an Underarm Turn.

Glance back at the pages describing the Throw-out and the Underarm Turn and you will see that the girl rejoins her partner by stepping forward, forward on the "quick-quick" count. The Sugar Foot Walk adds a variation to these counts.

A man must read the girl's part of the Sugar Foot Walk so that he will understand how to lead her. Study the entire facing page.

MAN'S PART

At the end of an open pattern, such as the Throw-out Break, instead of stepping back and forward on the "quick-quick" counts, step back, back.

As you do so, keep your left arm rigid so that you will have strong enough control to lean away from the girl and pull her toward you in her swishing, swiveling "Sugar" Walk.

The illustration on the facing page shows a girl practicing the Sugar Foot Walk without a partner. In actual dancing, the man would be pulling her by her right hand, held in his left hand.

GIRL'S PART, SUGAR FOOT

Read the facing page to understand your dance position and the counts used.

Lean back from your partner, extending your right arm rather rigidly.

1. Step forward with right foot, toes out and heel turned well in, immediately swiveling your foot in place and turning heel out (quick).
2. Same movement forward with left foot.

How to Use the Sugar Foot in a Continued Walk

As DESCRIBED so far, the Sugar Foot is merely a varied way to end an open step. In other words, the girl would be swiveling forward twice to join her partner and resume regular dance position.

The man can, however, continue the pattern of pulling the girl toward him in Sugar Foot styling instead of immediately resuming dance position.

To do so, he would walk backward in a circle to his right for six additional "quick" counts leading the girl to Sugar-Foot six times toward him. The man's sixth step would actually be taken in place so that he could bring the girl into closed position.

The Tuck-in Turn in Swing

MAN'S PART

1. Forward with left turning girl to step forward as shown in illustration No. 1 (slow).
2. Step in place with right leading girl into a complete turn to her right (slow). Illustration No. 2 shows girl about to be turned. (Man starts her turn with a pull of his right hand, then releases her entirely.)
3. Back on left and regain left hand hold of girl (quick).
4. Step in place with right, resuming regular dance position (quick).

GIRL'S PART

1. Take a Triple, starting with your right foot. (Illustration No. 1 shows position at finish of Triple.)
2. As man turns you sharply to your right, use a Triple, starting with your left foot. (Illustration No. 2 shows the beginning of this Triple — the left footstep has been taken. The remainder of the Triple will be taken while turning.)
3. Step back on right (quick).
4. Step forward on left (quick).

Part Eleven

ROCK 'N' ROLL

Rock 'n' Roll

Rock 'n' Roll is the newest variation of Swing — a bouncy, carefree dance usually associated in our minds with teen-agers. Steps vary in different localities, but this is the basic Rock 'n' Roll pattern that is used in most parts of the country.

Count slow, slow, quick, quick.

MAN'S PART

START

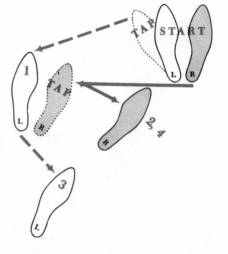

1. Tap almost in place with left toe, no weight, and then step to left side with left foot, turning slightly right (slow).
2. Tap right foot next to left, no weight, and then step to right side with right foot (slow).
3. Step back with left foot (quick).
4. Step forward with right foot (quick).

Style: On count 1, rock body forward as you tap with left toe; then roll back on heel as you step with left foot. On count 2, rock forward as you tap with right toes; roll back on heel as you step with right foot. When proficient, dance entire Basic Step turning right.

GIRL: Tap and step, as in man's part, but starting with right foot on count 1 and with left foot on count 2.

Step *back* with right foot on count 3; forward with left foot on count 4.

The Throw-out Break in Rock 'n' Roll

Look at the illustration of the Throw-out Break in Swing on page 200. This is the same *position* you will use for the Rock 'n' Roll Throw-out. Only the footwork is different.

MAN'S PART

First use one or more Basic Rock 'n' Roll Steps, either in place or turning right.

Continue the footwork of the Basic Step, but on the first "slow" release your right hand hold and lead the girl, by your left hand, into the Throw-out open position.

GIRL'S PART

Use Rock 'n' Roll Basic Step footwork as man "throws" you out into an open Break position.

The Sugar Push in Rock 'n' Roll

MAN'S PART

PRECEDE the Sugar Push with a Throw-out Break. As the girl steps forward on count 4 (quick), check her in open position, using a double hand hold. You are now ready for the Sugar Push pattern.

1. Tap and step with left foot, pulling girl into Right Parallel position with your left hand (slow). See Illustration No. 1.
2. Step forward with right foot, pulling girl into Left Parallel position with your right hand (slow). See Illustration No. 2.
3, 4. Rock back on left foot, rock forward on right foot (quick, quick) as you push girl into the open position shown in Illustration No. 3.

You may repeat the Sugar Push as many times as you wish. When ready to end the pattern, use a Basic Rock 'n' Roll Step, bringing girl into regular closed position on the "quick-quick" counts.

GIRL: Study the man's part carefully. If possible, practice this step with another girl and alternate leading and following.

1

2

3

Rock 'n' Roll Swivels

MAN'S PART

Precede the Swivels with a Throw-out Break. As the girl steps forward on count 4 (quick), check her in open position with a double hand hold (as at the start of Sugar Push).

You are now ready to lead the Swivels. These depend almost entirely *on both partners' using strong pressure with both hands to facilitate the swiveling body action.*

The Swivels are all "quick" counts.

1. Toe in with left foot, no weight on left, and *pull left hand back.* As you can see in Illustration No. 1, this swivels man's body to his right.
2. Heel in with left foot, no weight on left, and *push left hand forward.* As shown in Illustration No. 2, this swivels man's body to his left.
3. Cross left foot over right, weight on left, and *pull left hand back.* See Illustration No. 3.

4, 5, 6. Same action with right foot.

Repeat entire six counts for total of twelve "quicks."

GIRL: Your footwork is exactly like the man's except that you will swivel with your right foot first.

It is essential that you hold arms rather rigid, pressing both hands against the man's hands.

The Rock 'n' Roll Shuffle

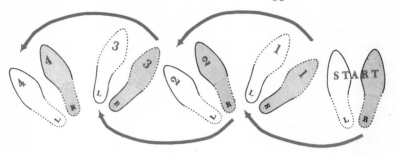

MAN'S PART

Precede with a Basic Rock 'n' Roll pattern *with this change:* Instead of stepping back, forward on the "quick-quick" counts, step in place with left foot, keeping weight on toes and bring right foot next to left, weight on right toes.

Your feet will now be in the position shown as "start" in the above diagram.

1. Twist both heels to the left, rocking weight back on heels.
2. Twist both toes to the left, rolling weight forward on toes.
Repeat for total of eight "quick" counts, progressing left.

LEAD: During the Basic Rock 'n' Roll Step that precedes the shuffle, hold girl firmly, so that she will not step back, forward on the "quick-quick" counts. Instead, your lead must keep her opposite you and "rocked" back with her weight on her heels.

GIRL: Read man's part and note that your feet will be together at the start of this step, weight on both heels.

1. Twist both toes to the right, rolling weight forward on toes.
2. Twist both heels to the right, rocking weight back on heels.
Repeat for eight counts, progressing right.

Part Twelve

DANCE SECRETS

By Kathryn Murray

How Many Steps Should a Good Dancer Know?

THERE IS no rule nor measure to determine the number of steps a good dancer should know. Step patterns in dancing are like words in conversation. When you have a fluent vocabulary, you can express yourself more easily and can hold a listener's interest more readily. The more words you have at your command, the more colorful your conversation. With a choice, you can select the exact, apt word to suit your meaning.

And so it is with steps in dancing. When you have mastered a wide variety of patterns, you can express yourself easily to any music, with any partner.

However, if you are a beginner, forget about *quantity* of steps for the time being. Instead, concentrate on *quality*. Practice each step thoroughly until you can dance it to any tempo and feel confident that you could lead it.

A girl should also avoid hasty study. She should follow the instructions given, learning the man's part before her own wherever specified. There is also a section on exercises for girls near the end of this book. Practiced faithfully, the exercises will produce remarkable results in muscular grace.

Once you have mastered the steps in this book, you will find it easy to add your own variations. You will not need a set routine; the music will actually tell your feet what to do.

So be content to build your repertoire of step patterns slowly. Review and perfect each carefully. Variety may be the spice of life but spice should be *added* to the completed product!

Dancing Don'ts

Don't hang your weight on your partner's arm.

Don't start off on the wrong foot.

Don't start off on the wrong foot! The man always starts with his left foot — the girl with her right. Easy? Sure, if you know your left from your right.

Don't (girls) hang your full weight on your partner's arm; he can't dance for both of you. Balance on your own two feet and support your own weight. If you can't, then stay home and take your vitamins.

Don't (men) walk forward all of the time. Your partner will get mighty tired of backing up all evening. Try strolling backward for five minutes straight and you'll get the idea.

Don't criticize your partner's dancing.

Don't make your back steps too short.

Don't criticize your partner's dancing. This goes for both sexes. Finding fault with the other fellow is a sure sign of a beginner — or, worse, of a sourpuss.

Don't (girls) always blame your crushed toe on your partner. Maybe your back steps are too short. Test yourself — are the toes of your new slippers soiled already? Then practice long steps, stretching back with your toes. Get out of his way!

Don't be a sad-eyed Sammy or a sour-apple Sue. The dance floor is a place for fun; do your worrying on your own time. Smile now, or you're apt to have no one to smile with.

Don't grip your partner's hand or thumb too firmly.

Don't dance with your hips 'way back.

Don't (girls) believe for a minute that all you have to do is relax. To relax is to collapse. Be alert, full of pep, on your toes — then you'll be fun as a partner!

Don't forget that the best position for dancing is the same as for walking — keep erect. Dancing with hips 'way back is out of date. Besides, remember the stag line's view; you owe something to your public!

Don't clutch your partner's hand too firmly. You may not know your own strength. And, girls, don't take a death grip on the poor man's thumb; you've got him safely hooked for the dance — he can't get away.

Don't be a butterfly.

Don't hum or sing loudly. Remember that you're only an inch from your partner's ear. Humming or singing is fine if you're good enough to compete with the orchestra. But if you aren't sure of the tune or the words, do your warbling in the shower.

Don't (girls) be butterflies. You have arms, not wings. A loose hold will make you miss the lead and stumble. What a come-down that will be! Hold your left hand in a firm grip on the back of your partner's shoulder — you'll keep your balance and your partner's praise.

Don't hug the floor! LIFT YOUR FEET! Lift your feet a fraction of an inch off the floor and move them through the air. Air offers no resistance — therefore, you can step lightly and effortlessly. Lift your feet slightly for graceful dancing.

Don't keep apologizing. When you make a mistake say, "I'm sorry" — but just say it once. If you protest, "Gee, I'm clumsy" too often, someone may believe you.

Don't go to extremes.

Don't go to extremes. A stately tread belongs in marble halls; bouncing high is for the village green. They are both too exaggerated for present-day dancing.

Dancers used to hop high in the days of the Gallop, Polka and Leaping Waltz. Then fashions changed and swung far the other way. Dancing became overly conservative, dignified. Every step seemed meticulously measured.

With this vogue for dignity, in about 1900, came the theory that good dancers must not lift their feet. Dancing teachers of the day preached, "Do not permit a crack of light to show between your feet and the floor."

This certainly made for dull dancing. How can you dance lightly, with expression and animation, when your feet scrape the floor? The answer is, you can't. So you must lift your feet while you dance, but take it easy.

How to Express Your Personality in Your Dancing

IN A WHOLE roomful of dancers, did you ever spot one person who you wished could be your partner? You'll notice that it isn't appearance alone that attracts you. There is another quality that draws your attention like a magnet. Call it "charm" or "personality"—however you describe it, it shows in everything you do.

You can develop that extra something that will make your dancing personality colorful, attractive. It's easy, once you know how to do it.

The trick is, accent your dancing! Give it highlights. Accent in dancing is a great deal like accent in speaking. A person who talks in a flat, level, unvarying voice is a bore to listeners. He may know a great deal and have a fine vocabulary at his command but it all goes to waste because of his dreary, droning voice.

A man may know a great variety of steps and yet be a dull dancing partner. He must learn to accent his dancing to give it life and pep. Girls, too, must accent the beat and rhythm of the music before they can dance with expression.

To accent in dancing, merely emphasize the same beat of the music that the orchestra does. You can find this most easily by listening for the bass drumbeats. Turn on your radio and listen. Note that in a Waltz the drummer strikes in measures of three beats but that he strikes hardest on each *first* beat.

Practice the Waltz, accenting or emphasizing the first of every three steps. Because a man always starts dancing with his left foot, his first accented step in the Waltz will be taken with his left. A girl will start accenting with her right foot.

It will take a few hours of practice before you can do this easily and automatically. But it's worth the time — it will make dancing more fun for you, more exciting to your partners and more attractive to onlookers.

How to Judge
Character by Dancing

As WE watch various couples walk out on the dance floor, we often think to ourselves, "I wonder what sort of people they are." Within a very few minutes we have our answer. For very quickly such traits as timidity, aggressiveness, consideration for others, arrogance, and such characteristics reveal themselves when people dance.

There are those who love themselves — can you spot them? They point their toes too gracefully and meticulously, stepping very carefully indeed. And why shouldn't they take good care of the ten little tootsies that are THEIRS!

The "cuddly couples" are fun to watch — unless you're related to them! Dance floor petters never outgrow the urge. You can put bells on their toes and wedding rings on their fingers — they'll still cuddle!

Here's one of masculine gender only. He meanders around the floor, pushing his partner into everything that comes his way. He's inconsiderate and thoughtless. Marry his type and life will be one traffic jam after another — with you as the bumper!

Then there are the "casual" ones. The girl with sloppy "I-don't-care" posture and the man jes' shufflin' along. She's probably a job-drifter hoping for the divine job with hours from twelve to one — and with an hour off for lunch. When she marries, she'll be a handy gal with a can opener. And her limping hazard? The world owes him a living — you might as well deliver it right to his door.

Know the brand marks of jealousy? The possessive man cups his hand tightly on his partner's back. His posture is crouching, as though ready for a springing pounce. Now, the trouble with a jealous gal is that her little ways are so fetching — at first. She clings to her partner's arm like glue, looks up in his eyes with an "aren't-you-wonderful" effect and is so attentive that she goes to his head. But, her husband will have a male secretary if she has anything to say!

Don't look too hard for the timid souls — they'll sink to the floor if you stare at them. The masculine variety has low-slung elbows, an apologetic manner, and a hangdog expression. He takes faltering steps and barely touches his partner. He's hard to

The cuddly couple

The timid souls

The aggressive couple

follow because he's too shy to lead. The girls of this type take uncertain steps, droop their arms and get an until-death-do-us-part grip on their partner's left thumb.

Beware of the bully — you can spot him on sight. He swings his partner around fast and furiously, with complete disregard for her clothes, hair and general well-being.

It takes all kinds to make a world — and you'll find one of each on every dance floor. Watch their steps!

The bully

The arrogant couple

The casual couple

Helpful Hints for Tall Girls

ONE CHARACTERISTIC that is admired in American girls is their height and fine bearing. Whereas most short girls yearn to be taller, few tall girls would trade places with them. Tall girls should be proud of their size; they should remember that models, who are selected for beauty of appearance, are always well above average height.

However, short men do avoid dancing with girls who tower above them. They are afraid of looking insignificant and comic — even when they secretly admire the girl's appearance.

Tall girls can be smart — they can seem shorter to partners whenever they choose. Here are two pointers that work:

1. KEEP YOUR ELBOWS LOW when you dance. You will appear shorter because your partners will not have to reach upward for dancing position. But practice this with your girl friends first so that you can avoid resting your arms heavily on your partner.
2. Without changing your natural standing posture in any way, LET YOUR KNEES BEND SLIGHTLY. This will reduce your height by several inches. Practice in private!

Perhaps you will feel that these suggestions do not improve your appearance. But, if I were a girl who had to choose between pleasing my partner or the onlookers, I wouldn't hesitate for a moment. I'd forget my appearance, if need be, and stand so that my partner would feel comfortable and would want to dance with me again.

DANGERS FOR TALL GIRLS TO AVOID

Tall girls should never try to appear smaller by leaning forward. This will make you difficult to lead, whether your partner is tall or short. Your hips and feet will be too far apart from your partner's and you will not only look but feel awkward in all steps. It is an impossible position in which to follow turning steps.

Do not take short steps. No matter how tall you are, you can never take too long a step. Don't worry — your partner's right hand will act as a safety brake.

Be proud of your height — and carry it proudly!

Keep your elbows low.

Let your knees bend slightly.

Helpful Hints for Small Girls

LITTLE GIRLS often complain about their lack of height — but they never remember the advantages they have. Just think of it — no partner is ever the wrong size. Men of all sizes are possible partners.

Even the smallest girl, whose vision is obscured by a man's tie, can be a comfortable, adjustable partner for a six-foot-plus. Here are confidential hints to pint-sizers:

1. Train yourself to dance on the tips of your toes instead of balancing your weight on the soles of your feet. Practice this, at home and alone, until you can stretch and reach smoothly.

2. Always imagine that you are trying to touch the ceiling with the top of your head. Stretch high up, from the waist, to gain height.

3. Here is the most valuable tip of all: LEAD WITH YOUR TOES! You can actually see in your mirror that by reaching back, with your big toe leading, you have lengthened your step from four to six inches. By doing this, your steps will be as long as those taken by a girl five inches taller than you are.

4. Hold your elbows as high as you can. Practice alone, holding your arms bent in partner position — as high up as possible. Exaggerate — and your muscles will be strengthened and ready for the real thing.

5. Always hold firmly with your left hand at the back of your partner's shoulder. No matter how hard you grip, it will be

welcome to him. Every man finds it easier to lead a girl who holds firmly to his right shoulder.

6. Never take short steps. Practice until you can step forward, backward and to each side with a long, graceful stride (toes leading).

Dance on the tips of your toes and take long steps.

THE LAW OF OPPOSITES

Here is a secret of showmanship that will help you to present an attractive dancing appearance. I call it the "Law of Opposites." It is also known as "Contrabody Motion."

When you step forward with either foot, bring your opposite shoulder slightly forward. Look at the picture — note that the girl is stepping forward on her left foot and is turning her right shoulder slightly forward.

Try this movement of the body, while walking toward your mirror. It will remind you of the graceful, controlled steps that a high-diver takes on a springboard. Follow the rule of opposites in your dancing — it gives strength and assurance to the personality that you show.

But you need more than grace of motion to attract partners. The face must dance, too. Remember this — you are not dressed for dancing until you put on a smile! Show the cheerful side of your character when you dance — it will be contagious to your partner and to everyone who watches.

Exercises to Improve Your Dancing

FOR GIRLS

AT EVERY newsstand you will find books of instructions for playing tennis, golf, swimming, and so on. This information is easy to read and digest — but do you feel that you could perform these muscular activities just by knowing about them?

Dancing deals with the muscles, too. You can pick up steps just by watching them, or reading their description, but you will have your knowledge in your head only. Your feet and your body cannot respond to your will and desire alone; your muscles must first be trained to obey your command.

Men who want to be good dancers must learn only their own part, and train their muscles to follow the steps they choose to do. But girls are in a different position — they must be able to follow many partners, some tall, some short, some with a great variety of intricate steps, some with a weak lead and faltering steps.

The way to become an alert, agile partner is to train your muscles to obey quickly and to strengthen them to support you in any direction you choose to move.

You cannot dance merely by wanting to — any more than you can be a fine tennis player just because you know the rules and know that the game is fun to play.

To practice sufficiently takes character and determination. It takes enthusiasm, too. If you really want to be a far better than average dancer, you will study these exercises carefully. They are a sure means of training your dancing muscles quickly and effectively. Remember, no one can do it for you, but once you've achieved your ambition to be an attractive, popular partner, everyone will envy you.

Here are eight exercises for girls. You will find it more entertaining to do them in front of your mirror, in time to music.

EXERCISE 1

Have you ever wondered why some girls look better standing than others do? Or, have you ever wished that you knew how to stand when someone takes your snapshot?

Count 1 of this exercise will give you the same standing posture that the best photographers' models use. Count 2 will give you the back-step technique of an exhibition dancer.

To make your feet look well as you stand, train your heels to always come together — as in the illustration. The toes should be turned out and the knees should touch each other. Look in your mirror!

On the count of one, bring your heels together so that your knees touch and your toes point outward. Now, on the count of two, kick your right foot as far back as possible — toe pointed out and leading. Return to correct position of count 1. Repeat this same movement with your left foot and continue in time to slow Fox Trot music.

EXERCISE 2

This exercise will train your feet and ankles to look attractive from both the side and back views. It will also teach you to automatically keep your feet in a straight line, with toes turned outward.

Place feet together as in start of Exercise 1. Step straight back with your right foot, toes leading and stretching from the ankle. Now step back, in the same manner, with your left foot.

Repeat this backward walk continuously around the room. Exaggerate the toe and ankle stretching to exercise the muscles. They will then carry you more easily in actual dancing.

EXERCISE 3

The illustration shows the finished product of this exercise. If you find it difficult to keep your balance, don't be discouraged — it merely proves that you need the practice. It will come easily after a few tries.

This is glamour training — it will develop supple muscles in your diaphragm and waistline.

Stand with your heels together, and your hands held loosely at your sides.

Step sideways on your right foot to the right, and draw your left foot behind the right, as you see in the illustration. At the same time, bring your arms and hands up in the position shown. Sway to the right.

Then step with your left foot to the left and bring your right foot up to and in back of your left. Sway to the left.

It is helpful to practice this to slow Waltz music, using three counts for each swaying movement — 1, 2, 3 to right; 4, 5, 6 to left.

EXERCISE 4

When you first try this exercise, you may feel insecure. If so, lean on the top of your dresser or on the back of a chair until you can hold your balance.

This movement will train you to hold your head up high and it will gracefully arch your back. A stiff, unyielding back makes a girl feel wooden to her partner.

Begin by standing erect, with your hands at your sides and your heels together. Then swing into the position shown in the illustration.

Repeat, swinging back on the other foot.

This can be practiced to slow Waltz music or by counting 1, 2, 3. Don't bring your feet together again until after the third beat.

Note that the toes of the back-swinging foot are leading — and pointing outward.

CAUTION: Do not repeat these exercises too often the first time — or you will regret it the next day!

EXERCISE 5

If you can do this exercise correctly, with your body erect, you will develop a good sense of equilibrium. Practice it until you are well satisfied with your appearance in your mirror.

Simply extend one foot to the side and raise it as high as possible as shown in the illustration. Note that — again — your toes should lead.

Practice this ten times with one foot and then repeat to the other side.

When you have mastered this, with good balance and keeping your body erect, then rise on the toes of the foot carrying the weight.

Count: 1, 2, 3, 4. Raise foot, 1, 2,. Lower foot, 3, 4. Try it to slow Fox Trot music.

This exercise will not only train you in balancing, but it will enable you to follow any quick side step that a partner may take.

EXERCISE 6

Do your knees crra-ack as you bend? You can oil them with this exercise — it's meant to overcome stiff knee joints. It will help you to take smooth dancing steps, rather than the jerky movements of a beginner.

To begin, stand up straight in a natural position.

Take a long forward step with your right foot and place the weight on that foot. Bend the right knee and, keeping your body erect, bend as far down as possible.

Not so easy? The results will be worth it — try again.

After bending, rise and resume your standing position. Now, without moving out of place, step forward with your left foot — weight on that foot — and bend as before.

Do this exercise gradually, a few times a day at first, or you may need rubbing oil for your knees!

If you are practicing to music, allow three beats of a Waltz for the downward bend and three beats to rise to place.

EXERCISE 7

Girls who are not good dancers always dread dancing forward, toward their partners. It makes them feel insecure, clumsy — and they are in fear of stumbling over the man's feet.

Good dancers must be able to glide forward easily. In the Waltz, for instance, almost half the girl's steps will be toward her partner. This exercise will give you the security and confidence that you need; practice it.

Without bending your body forward, raise your right foot until it is parallel with the floor. Stretch your toes out — not up.

To develop dancing poise, hold your foot up for about five seconds, then lower it slowly. Repeat ten times, then try it with the other foot.

EXERCISE 8

It puzzles a man when he finds that some big, stout girls are easy and light to lead — while a slender one-hundred-pounder may be as heavy as lead.

If you want to hear a man say to you, "You're wonderful to dance with — you're as light as a feather," then train your arms. This exercise will do it — and furthermore, it will add to your balance and poise.

Rise up on your right toe, raising your left leg backward, as high as you can. Let your toes lead and point outward. At the same time, bring your right arm up in the position shown in the picture. Hold this graceful pose for three beats of a Waltz measure, then slowly lower your hands and feet.

IMPORTANT: Always make your wrists lead when using your arms and hands.

"I have often said that if I were compelled to have one required subject in Harvard College, I would make it dancing if I could."*

— DR. CHARLES W. ELIOT

* From Henry James' *Charles W. Eliot*, Vol. II.

Part Thirteen

DANCE ETIQUETTE

Dance Etiquette

MANY PEOPLE seem to shy away from the word "etiquette." It has an old-fashioned sound. But etiquette, after all, is merely the practical application of good common sense and attractive manners.

Dancing is a partnership and group activity, and so it concerns other people besides yourself. There is never any excuse for faulty manners that might affect others or react on them. A popular member of a dancing group is considerate — and shows regard for the comfort and pleasure of partners, a hostess and the other guests.

Once you have accepted an invitation to a dance, you have automatically agreed to live up to the obligations it implies. You are expected to be suitably dressed, to be pleasant company and, above all, to be able to dance.

No one would dream of accepting an invitation for tennis or bridge unless he could play. But many will accept dancing dates when they know quite well that their dancing is not good enough for a partner to enjoy. It's odd, isn't it?

If you can't dance with confidence, have the courage to refuse dancing invitations. Wait until you have the ability and can appear in the best light possible. By starting to practice immediately, you'll be ready and in demand the next time!

A man who accepts an invitation to a dance cannot spend the entire evening with the one partner of his choice. By accepting, he has agreed to add to the festivity of the evening by mingling with the group, by asking several partners to dance, or by changing partners with other couples. Natural courtesy dictates the rule that he must seek out and invite his hostess to dance. If she has daughters or sisters present, they must not be overlooked.

A girl must wait to be asked to dance, but she has her obligations to the party. She cannot, for instance, refuse one partner and then turn around and accept another. Neither should a girl attempt to tie strings to a partner — to hold on to him. She must release him gracefully so that he can get about and dance with others.

When entering or leaving the dance room, the girl always precedes. Men never go first unless they need to do so to give assistance, such as in helping a girl out of a car, bus or so on.

It is no longer considered good taste for a man to take the girl's arm when they are walking to or from the dance floor. This has been out of date for years.

There is a right and wrong way to ask a girl to dance. It puts her in an awkward spot if you say, "Have you the next dance taken?" What girl wants to admit that her dances are not taken! Instead, say, "May I have the next dance?" Don't forget this, it holds true for all invitations. It is more polite to say, "Will you

Don't take the girl's arm when walking to or from the dance floor.

go dancing with me on Friday night?" than tactlessly to say, "What are you doing on Friday night?" See the difference?

At the end of each dance, a man must always escort his partner back to where she was sitting. He must never leave her in the middle of the floor. (But, don't forget, he doesn't have to take her by the arm to lead her off!)

When leaving a girl after dancing with her, a man should make some pleasant remark like "Thank you so much — I enjoyed dancing with you." He should be careful not to say, "I'll be back later," unless he plans to return. A man is well protected by the rules of etiquette. If he has had an uncongenial or dull partner, he can make his exit very smoothly by saying that he must find the girl with whom he has the next dance. Or that he has not yet danced with the hostess.

CUTTING IN

Cutting in is an acceptable custom at almost all dances that are held in America. If a man wants to cut in on the girl of his choice, he should wait until she is dancing fairly near him, at the outer

Cutting in is an acceptable custom.

Don't refuse to break
—it's bad form.

Don't pounce on a
new partner with
obvious delight.

edge of the floor. Then he can easily step to her side and nod pleasantly, saying, "May I?" to her partner.

It is considered childishly bad form to refuse to "break." Instead, the man who has been cut in on should step aside good-naturedly, with a slight bow and a smile, and join the stag line. From there, he can do a little cutting-in himself.

There is a generally accepted rule that there must be an intervening cut-in before a man can return to claim his original partner. For instance, if Bill cuts in on John, John should not cut back on Bill. He should wait until another man is dancing with the girl.

The cut-in system is very cruel to a girl. Even when she likes the partner she has, she yearns for cut-ins, to prove her popularity. But, no matter how welcome the cut is, a girl should not show undue glee. She should smile equally at her original partner and at her new one.

A girl who pounces on a new cut-in with obvious delight makes him wary and suspicious. Further, her stock goes down with a bang because she has been noticeably insulting to her original partner. Neither can she show reluctance to break, even when her original partner is her dream man. Girls must chart their course very carefully for smooth sailing.

CONVERSATION

This is a matter of personality, but there are general rules of good manners to consider. The first taboo is: Don't argue! Dancing is a partnership that depends on accord. Two people cannot move as one and enjoy the rhythm of the music together unless they feel harmonious toward each other. So, avoid subjects that might breed discord, such as politics, religion, school elections, and so on. Even when you discuss songs or bands, remember that the sweetest words ever spoken are: "I think you're right!"

There are some people who cannot talk as they dance. Theirs is a companionable silence because it is obvious that their minds are occupied with the rhythm of the music and the pleasure of the dance.

The strong, stern, silent man and the frosty-faced, forbidding female don't belong at a dance. Their partners find them un-

Don't look too stern.

Don't spend your dance arguing

Don't talk incessantly.

pleasant and the onlookers will avoid them. There may be some reason not to talk as you dance, but always keep your smile on!

The walkie-talkie chatterbox is a conversational hazard, too. There are always a few at every dance; they are so insecure or tense that they have forgotten that Silence Is Golden. Their chatter is so steady that it drowns out the loudest band. Like the brook, they ripple on and on. Nothing can be done about it, but you can profit by their example!

INTRODUCTIONS

Introducing people is a bugbear to those who are shy and to those who are young and unpracticed. Actually, the only difficult part is to remember names — and to have them at the tip of your tongue. Otherwise, your cues are easy: You always present the man to the girl, mentioning her name first: "Lillian, this is Mr. Brown — Miss Smith." Or, if you are not on first-name terms with her, you can say, "Miss Smith, may I present Mr. Brown."

When introducing two women, you present the younger one to the older: "Mrs. Jones, this is Miss Smith." If they are of equal age, it doesn't matter which name is mentioned first. "Mrs. Jones — Mrs. Brown."

ACKNOWLEDGING INTRODUCTIONS

It is good training to make a point of remembering names; therefore many people form the habit of acknowledging introductions by repeating the name: "How do you do, Mrs. Brown." If you have not really heard the other person's name, it will flatter them to have you say, "Did you say Mrs. Brown? How do you do."

Don't make the famous mistake that was made by a young girl, who was too shy to ask to have the name repeated — and who, later in the evening, asked, "I'm not quite sure — how do you spell your name?" "S-M-I-T-H, plain Smith," he replied.

Certain replies to introductions have fallen into too common usage and are not considered good taste. As an example: "Pleased to meet you" is no longer used. Yet "I'm so glad to know you" is quite acceptable.

A woman does not rise to acknowledge introductions, unless she is the hostess, or is being introduced to an older person. A hostess rises to greet all of her guests, men or women.

NIGHT CLUB DANCING

So far, we have discussed private dancing parties.

A restaurant featuring dancing is quite different. Here your

Avoid complicated steps on a small dance floor.

only obligation is to the people of your own party. A cut-in from a stranger should never be accepted, nor should it be offered. A man should avoid leaving his date alone at the table unless it is really necessary. Otherwise, she may be subjected to unwelcome attention.

Most restaurant and night-club dance floors are tiny in size, so in consideration of your partner and your neighbors, you should avoid complicated steps. Dance simply and follow the Line of Direction. This means to progress around the room counter-clockwise. Shorten your steps to fit the limitation of space.

ONE LAST WORD

It is not bad manners to suggest sitting down before the dance is over — that is, if you suggest the idea tactfully. Either partner can say, "It's warm in here, don't you think so? Shall we sit out and cool off for a few moments?" Or, "It's crowded, isn't it? I'm anxious to talk to you anyway — shall we sit down?"

From now on, try to think more kindly of the word "etiquette" — it protects you, too; don't you think so?

Part Fourteen

DANCING FOR CHILDREN

Why Children Should Learn to Dance

WHEN I first began to teach ballroom dancing, I had a class of twenty children in Atlanta, Georgia. How that class grew to a thousand — the largest in the world — is another story; but it was those years of experience that taught me how valuable an asset social dancing is to children.

Mothers and fathers have only a partial picture of their children's lives. For a complete view they would have to observe what happens in the classroom and the playground. Only then could they tell whether their children have confident young personalities or are so shy that they stumble over their lessons and edge away from games.

There is nothing more pathetic than the child who stands wistfully looking on while other boys and girls are playing — anxious, eager and envious, and yet afraid to join in when asked.

That child longs for the bell calling him back to class. But in the schoolroom timidity can result in a more serious failure. A timid child is apt to be tongue-tied, too embarrassed to show that he knows his lesson. Poor grades in school are often the result of shyness.

Every expert in child psychology will tell you that the child who doesn't mix needs self-confidence above all else. But self-confidence cannot be forced on a child — it must be developed. To feel physically relaxed, to be well poised in the company of other children, is the first important step.

To achieve this, ballroom dance training offers unique advantages. It is a rhythmic exercise that adds lithe, graceful muscular movement. And, since it is both a partnership and a group recreation, it simplifies social contacts during the formative years that set a pattern for the future. A child who has learned ballroom dancing gains not only improved posture and co-ordination but ease in relationships with companions.

It is not only the child with a shy appearance who will profit from ballroom dancing. Most children of the other extreme — those who act too self-assertive — have merely adopted that veneer to cover their own brand of insecurity. They, too, need surety and confidence if they are to get along well with people and be popular with friends.

The natural courtesies of the dancing class are acquired painlessly by each young member. Once instilled, those ingredients of good manners are never forgotten. Ballroom dancing offers more than mere steps — it includes charm of manner and consideration for others.

I do not believe that there must be an unavoidable stage in life called the "awkward age." When children are self-conscious and act either shy or swaggering, it is a grave mistake to take it for granted that they will outgrow their social handicap. Added years are not the cure, nor can time erase unfortunate memories. The cause of the so-called "awkward age" is lack of confidence. Left unaided, this can well become an enduring trait for life.

Dancing is but one means of instilling graceful body co-ordination, but it is the only muscular activity that brings social ease. A girl who has learned to be a good ballroom dancer as a child never fades into a wallflower. A boy who can dance is spared from many agonies of teen-age self-consciousness.

Children who dance well are popular!